The FRED OPERT STORY

Peter R Hill

Bon vivant, racing-car champion, entrepreneur, wheeler-dealer and champion-maker – this is the fascinating story of the irrepressible, effervescent Fred Opert. The man who brought European formula racing to America, and an American team to Europe

"He was a racer at heart, and he liked drivers who were racers;
who would give everything."
Marco Tolama

"He was such a character. You almost forgot you were paying him!"
Carl Liebich

Also from Veloce Publishing:

Biographies
A Chequered Life – Graham Warner and the Chequered Flag (Hesletine)
Amédée Gordini ... a true racing legend (Smith)
André Lefebvre, and the cars he created at Voisin and Citroën (Beck)
Bunty – Remembering a gentleman of noble Scottish-Irish descent (Schrader)
Chris Carter at Large – Stories from a lifetime in motorcycle racing (Carter & Skelton)
Cliff Allison, The Official Biography of – From the Fells to Ferrari (Gauld)
Edward Turner – The Man Behind the Motorcycles (Clew)
Driven by Desire – The Desiré Wilson Story
First Principles – The Official Biography of Keith Duckworth (Burr)
Inspired to Design – F1 cars, Indycars & racing tyres: the autobiography of Nigel Bennett (Bennett)
Jack Sears, The Official Biography of – Gentleman Jack (Gauld)
Jim Redman – 6 Times World Motorcycle Champion: The Autobiography (Redman)
John Chatham – 'Mr Big Healey' – The Official Biography (Burr)
The Lee Noble Story (Wilkins)
Mason's Motoring Mayhem – Tony Mason's hectic life in motorsport and television (Mason)
Raymond Mays' Magnificent Obsession (Apps)
Pat Moss Carlsson Story, The – Harnessing Horsepower (Turner)
'Sox' – Gary Hocking – the forgotten World Motorcycle Champion (Hughes)
Tony Robinson – The biography of a race mechanic (Wagstaff)
Virgil Exner – Visioneer: The Official Biography of Virgil M Exner Designer Extraordinaire (Grist)

WSC Giants
Audi R8 (Wagstaff)
Ferrari 312P & 312PB (Collins & McDonough)
Gulf-Mirage 1967 to 1982 (McDonough)
Matra Sports Cars – MS620, 630, 650, 660 & 670 – 1966 to 1974 (McDonough)

Those Were The Days ... Series
Alpine Trials & Rallies 1910-1973 (Pfundner)
Anglo-American Cars from the 1930s to the 1970s (Mort)
Brighton National Speed Trials (Gardiner)
British Drag Racing – The early years (Pettitt)
British Touring Car Racing (Collins)
Café Racer Phenomenon, The (Walker)
Drag Bike Racing in Britain – From the mid '60s to the mid '80s (Lee)
Endurance Racing at Silverstone in the 1970s & 1980s (Parker)
Hot Rod & Stock Car Racing in Britain in the 1980s (Neil)
Motor Racing at Brands Hatch in the Seventies (Parker)
Motor Racing at Brands Hatch in the Eighties (Parker)
Motor Racing at Crystal Palace (Collins)
Motor Racing at Goodwood in the Sixties (Gardiner)
Motor Racing at Nassau in the 1950s & 1960s (O'Neil)
Motor Racing at Oulton Park in the 1960s (McFadyen)
Motor Racing at Oulton Park in the 1970s (McFadyen)
Motor Racing at Thruxton in the 1970s (Grant-Braham)
Motor Racing at Thruxton in the 1980s (Grant-Braham)
Superprix – The Story of Birmingham Motor Race (Page & Collins)

www.veloce.co.uk

First published in May 2020 by Veloce Publishing Limited, Veloce House, Parkway Farm Business Park, Middle Farm Way, Poundbury, Dorchester DT1 3AR, England. Tel +44 (0)1305 260068 / Fax 01305 250479 / e-mail info@veloce.co.uk / web www.veloce.co.uk or www.velocebooks.com.
ISBN: 978-1-787115-65-1; UPC: 6-36847-01565-7.

The FRED OPERT STORY

VELOCE PUBLISHING
THE PUBLISHER OF FINE AUTOMOTIVE BOOKS

Peter R Hill

Contents

Forewords

Fred was an absolute racing fanatic, always telling the old stories about how it was with my dad back in the '70s. He was one of my greatest supporters, and once escaped hospital – without the approval of the doctors – to travel around the world to watch me race in Hungary ... I even had to send him all my reports from all the races when I was go-karting. He requested them, and was always giving me advice on them because I was also sending them to Ron Dennis. He was really always there supporting and guiding me. He was one of the great characters of motor racing – it's good that the story of his fascinating life has been told.

Nico Rosberg, World Champion 2016

Fred Opert was a super bloke, a real racer. He always had a big smile. I really enjoyed the few occasions I drove for him, particularly at Trois-Rivières in Canada, where we came second to Villeneuve and ahead of James Hunt.

Fred led an exciting life. It makes for a great story.

Alan Jones MBE, World Champion 1980

Fred and I experienced so much together. Through him I got to know so many wonderful people around the world.

I raced for him literally all over the globe, from our wonderful early times together in New Zealand (which were the best times in motorsport for Fred and me), through Europe, USA, Canada, Macau, and Japan. They were exhausting but exciting times, as we spent more time on airplanes than on the ground. I have a deep feeling of gratitude, as I knew there were times when he really couldn't afford to run me in his cars. However, he somehow always found a way to pay the bills!

He also was the best 'travel agent' on earth – during the era with no online booking, no internet or even fax!

Fred was a colourful character and one of the best-connected people in international single-seater motorsport. In his later years he also became the most devoted 'fan' of my son Nico in Formula One.

His love for racing, adventures and misadventures make great reading.

'Keke' Rosberg, World Champion 1982

The Defining Day

On a warm day in June 1963, a young second-year student from the New York University School of Law sat among criminals in the shared cell of a New York jail.

Fred Opert had a love of cars – *fast* cars – and this was what had landed him in jail. Several weeks previously he had been travelling at speed in his Jaguar XK150S, desperate not to miss a race meeting. Instead, he was stopped by the police and given a ticket.

Opert might have ignored the ticket, or perhaps he simply forgot about it when he went on vacation, visiting his parents in Massachusetts. Regardless, when the 24-year-old returned to the university, the police were waiting for him and he was arrested for not paying his fine. In court Opert was found guilty and fined $150 "plus five." He attempted to make a payment of $155, thinking the court had fined him "$150 plus $5" (equivalent to $1,307 in 2020, which Opert might have considered a serious fine but not *too* bad). To his horror he discovered that the "plus five" was five days in jail.

This was to be a defining week in his life. Friends brought him books to study, but while in jail he missed a critical exam. The seriousness of his situation caused him to reflect on what he wanted to do with his life, and to make a decision about what his real love and priorities were. There would have been the pressure of knowing that his father had wanted to be an attorney, but had given up his studies in favour of financial security for his family. Yet perhaps his missed exam could have been fate opening the door on a life of pursuing his first love, cars and racing.

A short time later, without telling his parents, he gave up his law studies and started his career in the motor trade and motorsport – a career that would see Fred Opert become one of the most influential, well-respected, and well-liked people in motor racing around the globe in the '60s and '70s.

Fred Opert, through his company Fred Opert Racing, went on to influence the careers of at least 20 Formula One drivers, including three world champions. It wasn't only his drivers who benefited; Fred Opert Racing mechanics and team members went on to become some of the sport's best engineers and team owners.

It's possible that Keke Rosberg would not have become world champion if Opert hadn't been sent to jail. The careers of many other champion drivers might have been less successful – drivers like Alan Jones, Alain Prost, Bobby Rahal, Jacques Laffite, Didier Pironi, Jean-Pierre Jarrier, Jean-Pierre Jaussaud, Héctor Rebaque, Rolf Stommelen, and Rupert Keegan, all of whom drove for Fred Opert Racing at pivotal times in their careers.

It is the opinion of family and friends that Opert would have made a very good attorney, but a fast Jaguar and a speeding ticket robbed the law profession of his talents and gave motorsport one of its most interesting characters.

When the young Fred Opert walked out of that New York prison in 1963, the excitement and glamour of a life in motorsport were still a few years away. Nevertheless, these were upbeat, optimistic times in the USA and England. The Beatles had bounced onto the world stage, and would shortly ride a wave of hysterical teenage adulation in the USA after appearing on the Ed Sullivan show. The bad boys of rock, The Rolling Stones, would reintroduce white Americans to their own country's blues music; Sean Connery stole many hearts as James Bond in Goldfinger; and Ford USA had its own hit with the Mustang.

At the Indianapolis 500 that year, Scotsman Jim Clark had sent shudders through the front-engined roadster establishment when he came a close second in his "itty bitty" rear-engined Lotus. The race was controversially won by Parnelli Jones, his roadster trailing oil that failed to attract a black flag. Jack Brabham had previously set the rear-engine revolution in motion in 1961 with a Cooper T54, and the final nail was hammered into the front-engine roadsters' coffin in 1965 when Jim Clark won the Indianapolis Borg Warner trophy in a Lotus-Ford.

The English weren't just turning the world of rock & roll on its head, they were also producing light, agile sports cars and racing cars that would soon dominate the starting grids of races the world over. This was an ideal environment for the ever-smiling, ever-positive, talented, entrepreneurial and resourceful Fred Opert.

His Destiny – Motorsport and Automobiles

E
ven when he was at law school, Opert worked for an auto sales company. This was Johnson Motors, in Port Washington on Long Island; a dealership that sold British cars, primarily makes from UK company The Rootes Group – such as Hillman, Humber, Singer and Sunbeam – which was progressively taken over by the Chrysler Corporation in the mid-'60s.

Opert grew up in Worcester, Massachusetts, about 40 miles west of Boston. The city was home to many groups of immigrants. His love of cars came from his family of Polish Jewish immigrants who had settled in Worcester, where Opert's father, Sam, had a clothing store. A young Fred Opert helped out in the store. By coincidence his father had also dropped out of law school, but in completely different circumstances.

Sam Opert left St John's University School of Law in New York because he couldn't afford to continue his studies during the depression. Ironically, he ended up in Worcester because Boston University had a satellite law school there, so he thought he could continue his degree at a less expensive institution while he worked. When he got to Worcester, Boston University closed the law school annex, and, as a result, he ended up in the retail business and never was able to return to law.

Sam Opert managed several hosiery stores in New York City (women's hosiery was a very lucrative business at that time). Before buying his own store in Fitchburg, Massachusetts, he accepted a position as the manager of a chain of women's department stores in the mid-west, Wisconsin and Illinois. He left Worcester by himself to start working in that position. The Opert children, Fred, Larry and Judi, were still in school in Worcester.

Sam purchased a home for the family in Springfield, Illinois. However, his wife Ida decided that she couldn't move that far away from her own family (she was one of 11 children) and she convinced him to sell the new house, quit his job and come back home. He did, then purchased his own store in Fitchburg.

Sam made the most of his business opportunities, and was successful, but he always regretted not finishing his law studies – to the point where, late in his life, he applied to complete his degree. Sadly, no law school would accept his previous credits.

His success at running the family's clothing store provided him with the opportunity to enjoy his own love of automobiles. Fred Opert's sister, Judi, recalls that there were always interesting cars in the family, including several Chrysler Hemi 300s, a Plymouth Sport Fury, a Cadillac, and her mother's Ford Thunderbird.

Fred's first car was an MGA that his father bought for him at the start of his sophomore semester at the University of Virginia, in 1958. The MGA was to be replaced with the silver 1959 Jaguar XK150S that was responsible, in a number of ways, for his motor racing career.

As well as being the initiator of Fred's interest in cars, Sam Opert was a great supporter of his son's career, despite the circumstances under which it started. Fred was an equally devoted son who shared his passion with his parents, attending races with his father.

Fred was 20, and his sister just 15, when he got the Jaguar XK150S. He attended the Sports Car Club of America (SCCA) New England drivers' school and went racing. His parents were initially unaware of his racing, as he took Judi along as a smokescreen; they thought how nice it was that brother and sister went out on day trips in the Jaguar. Fred had a roll bar that he could remove from the car quite easily and hide in the trunk, so his parents wouldn't find out what he was up to.

His sister Judi was equally enthusiastic:

"Freddie always got me weird cars – who had heard of an Elva Courier in the USA in 1964? – but I was driving one. My first car was an Austin Healey. I'd never driven a car with a stick shift, but Freddie delivered the car to me in New York and left me to it. When I turned 50 he turned up with what became my first Porsche 911."

During Opert's junior year at the University of Virginia (UVA) he started drag racing the Jaguar at several of Virginia's drag strips. He earned trophies for winning his class (C sports) at each event he competed in. However, at the end of the first semester of his senior year at UVA a somehow low score in French had put him on academic probation. This was ironic, given that he later became something of a Francophile, was heavily involved with French racing drivers, and gained sponsorship from the French Gitanes brand of cigarettes.

This probation resulted in a directive from UVA to remove his car from campus, due to a rule that a student could not have a car on campus during a probation semester.

Opert's brother Larry takes up the story:

"Fred did not want our parents to know about either the academic probation or the directive for him to remove the Jag from campus. At the time, I was a freshman at the University of Vermont (UVM) in Burlington. Fred called me, told me about his predicament, and we came up with a plan: he would drive the Jag to Boston, I would take a bus to Boston, meet him at the bus station, drive the Jag back to Burlington, and he would take a bus back to Charlottesville. After his graduation in May he would come to Burlington and retrieve his car. I agreed, and we both immediately started out for Boston."

9

There was a problem with the plan, as freshmen were not allowed to have cars at UVM. So Larry kept the Jag hidden under a tarp behind his fraternity house, only driving it on weekends for forays up to Montreal, or across the State line to New York with friends, where the drinking age was only 18 as opposed to 21 back in Vermont. Then disaster struck.

In early May Larry decided to take the Jag out for a drive, squeezing two of his fraternity brothers into the two-seater. One perched on the transmission tunnel. They were enjoying the wind in their hair on a two lane road when an oncoming inebriated woman drove over the centre line, striking the Jag head on. The guy on the transmission tunnel was cut up where he hit the windscreen, while Larry and the other passenger were saved from injury by their belts. The Jag sustained the most damage and was towed back to UVM where it could once again hide under a tarpaulin.

At the time of the accident, Opert had graduated from UVA and just moved to an apartment in Boston, sharing with another graduate. They would both start law school together at Boston College in September.

Larry Opert describes the Jaguar recovery operation and its transformation into a competitive racing car:

"Fred and his roommate drove up to Burlington with a car trailer, loaded the Jag, and hauled it back to Boston. The car was first taken to a body shop to repair the damage, then to a racing performance shop where engine work was performed, and a roll bar fitted, plus other parts needed to comply with the rules and enable it not only to enter, but be competitive in a SCCA production class.

"Fred then went to SCCA's drivers' school with the Jag, obtained his initial SCCA regional racing license, then his national racing license. This was the start of what would prove to be a successful racing career, first as a sports car driver, then as a Formula C and B driver."

While living and studying in New York, Fred Opert purchased and raced an Austin Healey Sprite. In a smart move he secured a part-time job with a BMC (British Motor Corporation) dealer. This not only paid a wage, but more importantly it allowed him to buy parts for the Sprite at dealer cost. Sadly, the Sprite met an untimely end when Opert was racing it at Lime Rock Park. He hit a car that spun in front of him and wrote off his little car. To add insult to injury, he had to hitchhike back to New York, as he had driven the Sprite to the Connecticut track.

After he abandoned his law studies Opert moved to Chicago, where he worked for Carl Haas selling Elva and Lotus cars. But Opert was keen to be independent, so he moved back to New York where he operated out of a girlfriend's apartment for a while, selling sports car accessories while he started to import and deal in single seater formula race cars.

In 1965, age 26, he established Fred Opert Racing Enterprises and took premises in Palisades Park in New Jersey.

Entrepreneur and America's Leading Race Car Dealer

Rick Mansfield, who was to become one of Opert's first employees, joining him in 1966, describes his visit to the New York apartment from which Opert was selling automotive accessories: wheels, steering wheels, mufflers, gear knobs, and all the bits and pieces that appealed to young guys with sports cars.

"I bought a sports muffler from him. I had a MkII Sprite. He gave me an address in Manhattan, so I proceeded to go there and parked the car. I'm walking along the street and on a trailer was an Elva Courier, and underneath it was a pair of legs: it was his mechanic, Tom Wagner, who's working on it.

"I proceeded up two, three or four floors, and as I'm getting up the stairway there's mufflers, and wheels, and whatever, stacked. I thought, 'this guy's pretty trusting.' I knock on the door and go in, and I was very impressed to begin with because it looked like there were ladies' undergarments everywhere. It turned out that Opert was working out of his girlfriend's apartment.

"We got talking, and he was opening a shop, a retail outlet over in New Jersey. He said, 'Can you type?' and I said, 'Yeah, I can type fairly well, I did typing at high school.' So he offered me a job. He said he wanted someone who could type letters and run the parts department, and this and the other thing.

"I was maybe 20 years old at the time and I ran into this guy who bounced on the balls of his feet, and he offered me a job to work for this racing organisation. This didn't go over very big at home, because I was supposed to go to school full-time in up-state New York."

Opert's first business premises was an old barbershop at 171, Route 4, Palisades Park, New Jersey. An unlikely premises for a motor business. Mansfield described it as about the width of two jail cells, about 30 feet across and very long. He remembered him and Opert leaving the new premises with a car and trailer to drive back to Manhattan. They went to an office building where they met up with Opert's girlfriend, took a large metal filing cabinet from the office, dragged it down the stairs and tied it to the trailer. They returned to Palisades Park with their first piece of office furniture.

The old barbershop had a garage door at the back that, after a set of ramps was welded-up, allowed racing cars to be parked nose to tail, with one on display at the front. And so, the first of Fred Opert's business premises was created. Sometime later he rented a large garage close by to serve as a storeroom for the wheels and accessories that he was buying in bulk.

Before establishing his own business, Opert had started his life in motor car dealing by seeking dealerships for the English sports car, the Elva Courier. He was working for Carl Haas, who had a dealership in Chicago and was the USA importer for Elva cars from the UK. Opert's association with English sports cars continued over the next few years as he sold, drove and raced Elva Couriers.

Elva was a small British company started after the Second World War by Frank G Nichols. After initially producing racing cars – sports and Formula Junior – in 1958, the company built its first sports car that was suitable for both road and track. This was the Elva Courier, the car that would play an important part in Opert's early years as a car dealer and racer. The early Couriers had MGA 1500cc engines and gearboxes. When the Elva company suffered financial difficulties, Trojan (which would later build McLaren's customer race cars) bought the rights to the Courier and took over production.

Elva's original distributor had failed to pay for delivered cars, causing financial problems for the company, and it was when Elva went bankrupt that Carl Haas became involved. Haas recovered impounded cars, and then sold, or helped to sell, some of the cars that were owned by Elva. He also helped Frank Nichols to continue designing and building racing cars. When Nichols established the new Elva Cars (1961) Ltd, Haas took a financial interest and became the USA distributor for Elva Couriers. After Haas moved on to other agencies – principally Lola – Opert became the Elva importer. He also sold performance parts for the Couriers designed by Robert Gaunt.

In the summer of '64 Opert drove a new, silver Elva Courier MkIV T–Series roadster to a number of car dealerships to persuade some of them to take on Elva franchises. One of these dealerships was Ed Roth & Son in Glassboro, New Jersey.

Fred Schuchard, who worked for Ed Roth & Son, remembers Opert as "... extremely friendly, well-informed regarding his 'product,' low key and just a genuinely nice person. We formed an instant friendship ... Fred introduced himself as the area sales representative for Elva cars under the auspices of Carl Haas."

Val Roth owned the dealership, and after he and many of his staff test drove the Elva they signed up to be a dealer and ordered their first car.

Opert wasn't afraid to spend money to promote his company and its products. He had a stand at the New York Motor Show in 1964, where the car he had driven to Ed Roth & Son was displayed. In '65 Opert called Fred Schuchard and sold him this same display car. Schuchard had already met his future wife Connie when she bought an Elva Courier from the Roth dealership. It became quite a family affair as Connie's brother also purchased an Elva.

Throughout his life Opert kept in touch with people, and this often resulted in more business; and so it was with Schuchard. In '65 Opert once again called his friend to tell him that the London Auto Show Elva was being imported into the USA, and he described all its special attributes. Ed Roth & Son ordered the car, which Schuchard's future wife would fall in love with:

"When this car arrived at Ed Roth & Son, Connie fell in love with it and bought it, selling her 1964 Elva to her younger brother, Joe. Fred Opert gave us a slightly discounted price on this car, with a stipulation: we must allow him to exhibit the car in the upcoming International Automobile Show in New York City. Connie agreed enthusiastically, which led to Fred inviting us to drive the car up to New York and help him man his booth at the show.

"His booth, along with Connie's Elva, also had a Formula Junior open-wheeled race car on exhibit. This was my first encounter with Fred as proprietor of Fred Opert Racing Enterprises, his personal business."

So Opert was back at the New York Motor Show, with willing helpers who had agreed to let him use their car for display. This was a very smart deal for Opert, in which everyone was happy and he didn't have money tied up in a show car.

Elvas also became race cars for Opert and his brother Larry, who recalls their adventures in the cars:

"They were really fun cars ... I owned two of them. Fred and I had a secret course on an obscure public roadway, with few cops and zero traffic, where we raced Elvas against each other."

No doubt these informal races with his brother were practice for the serious racing that Opert was involved in, driving Elva Couriers. He went on to contest the 1966 Sebring 12-hour and Daytona 24-hour races, partnering with William McKemie.

As well as the Elva Couriers, Rick Mansfield remembered them dealing Elva BMWs and the first McLaren-Elvas. Mansfield made up a tee shirt with the Kiwi logo on the front; on the back was the word 'McLaren' followed by 'Elva, Elva, Elva,' all the way down. These proved to be very popular, "I was selling those as fast as we could make them."

Mansfield looked after the business in Opert's absence. On one occasion a guy walked in who, at first sight, appeared to Mansfield to be a hobo. He wandered around looking at what was available and then asked for Opert. Mansfield told him that Fred was away. He asked the man what sort of car he had, and told him they had steering wheels and gear knobs, but the stranger told him he was looking for a race car. He left his number and asked Mansfield to get Opert to call him.

"When Fred came back I said, 'This guy came in and wants to buy a race car.' Fred said, 'what's his name?' I told him, 'Fred Ashplant,' and Fred said, 'I hope you were nice to him, his father owns a bank in Nova Scotia.'"

Ashplant became one of Opert's paying drivers, and in 1967 was a contender for the SCCA Formula B Northeast Division title. He finished third, ahead of Joe Grimaldi who was another early Opert employee at the barbershop.

Opert's business continued to grow and flourish. Opert and Pierre Phillips, who operated on the west coast, were the two who started to bring small formula cars into the country – namely Brabhams, some Lotus, and Formula Two and Formula Three cars from Europe. Opert was instrumental in getting the Formula B & C Pro series started. In the beginning it was amateur, but with Opert's commitment to race car imports it grew. Of the new formula cars that were coming into the USA, the majority came in through Fred Opert Racing.

In the early days in Palisades Park, Opert had Tom Wagner and Joe Grimaldi working for him along with the young Rick Mansfield. Tom Wagner was a talented mechanic, and once the business grew he drove the Valvoline tractor/trailer carrying customers' race cars to race meetings. Despite only having sight in one eye, he proved to be a very quick racer after he left Opert. For a short time he had a race shop not far from Opert, before he went to work for Koni in Virginia.

By 1966 Opert was buying secondhand racing cars from the UK. He purchased copies of the UK magazine *Autosport* then combed through the classified advertisements looking for cars he could import and sell. The cars were shipped to the USA by boat, where the longshoremen would be bribed to ensure their safe passage off the dock, before being parked under the bridge on the Western Highway, where they were safe because most people had no idea what they were and no incentive to steal them.

Joe Grimaldi joined Opert in 1966. He was closer to Opert's age than Mansfield, and became involved in the sales of sports and racing cars. By this time Opert claimed to be America's leading race car dealer, a tag line that he included on his marketing material. Grimaldi recalls:

"I met Freddie because I bought a car from him. He was the Elva dealer for Carl Haas. I bought a race car from him – a used Elva Mk7. It was a pushrod car. It was terrible, I couldn't stand it, because I raced a D-Type Jaguar for a very long time. Anyway, I bought that from him and then I went to work for him. Then I bought an Elva Mk7S that had a Porsche engine in it [a 1700cc flat-four]. I put a twin-cam Ford in it and that was a really good car, and I went in the national championship in that car. I sold a couple of Mk8 Elvas when I was there."

Grimaldi also raced some of the formula cars that Opert imported.

Grimaldi and Opert had a fiery relationship, with the diminutive Italian always willing to argue with his boss. Mansfield witnessed the fireworks.

"He and Joe would fight like cats and dogs over everything. Joe would sell a car and Fred would say 'you didn't get enough money,' and things like that. Well at one point, Joe had the tow car, he had a Ford Wagon that was a four-speed. Joe got mad at him and took off, like on Thursday afternoon [before a race meeting], with the tow car. Fred didn't have anything to tow with. So then there was a whole negotiation over the phone."

One of their early race weekends went really badly. Fred had a double-decker open trailer to carry his and Grimaldi's Formula B Brabhams. They left the shop and headed for Bridgehampton, which was located on Long Island. When Mansfield came in the shop on Monday he found one car was a twisted wreck. He envisaged a terrible accident, with one of the drivers having rolled the car up into a ball, but it turned out that someone (or both of them?) had forgotten to tie the car down, and it fell off on the George Washington Bridge that goes from New Jersey to New York. They never made it to Bridgehampton.

Opert and Grimaldi also raced together as co-drivers in long distance and Trans-Am races. It was not a happy arrangement.

In 1968 the two raced a 911 Porsche under the Valvoline/Opert Racing entry in the Daytona 24-hour. They finished in 26th place, after starting from 45th. Grimaldi wasn't happy with his boss and co-driver:

"Freddie and I ran the Porsche together, a 911 from Valvoline in the Trans-Am [racing series]. We co-drove, which was not a pleasant experience actually. The first race we went to was Daytona for the 24-hours, and I qualified the car pretty good for a 911. Freddie, who had been driving it the year before, said 'you can't be faster than me,' so he went out and bent all the valves because he missed a shift. My mechanic and I, we took the head off the car in the infield and we started the race two hours late. They allowed you a two-hour period to fix the car.

"At mid-Ohio I qualified the car, I think fourth or fifth on the grid, when they were running the big cars and the little cars. Freddie says, 'I'm gunna start the race,' and on the first lap he over-revved it. I wanted to kill him."

Their business and racing relationship finally came to an end after an argument boiled over and Grimaldi punched Opert.

"I punched him in the nose one time. I think that's when I left him. He said something to me, and I got up and I punched him, and I walked out. I remember he came home to my wife and he told her I was crazy ... Anyway, he could be very aggravating. As a person, Fred was alright, but he wanted everybody else to do things for him, he was good at that."

Grimaldi left Fred Opert Racing in 1970. Later, he set up The Race Shop in competition with Opert, and became the March importer in partnership with Doug Shierson. The men must have remained on cordial terms, as Opert bought a March from Grimaldi in 1979 – after he had stopped importing Chevrons and was in the final year of running cars for USA customers.

To finance his race car purchases from England, Opert bought and exported American muscle cars. Opert's employees, and even his paying drivers, were called on to help with these exports. They would go in convoy to car dealers in New York to pick up Camaros, Firebirds and Mustangs that Opert had purchased, then drive the cars to the docks ready for shipping to the UK. The trunks of these cars often carried car parts to which the dock workers chose to turn a blind eye. The UK sterling amounts that came from the sale of the muscle cars and parts paid for the race cars Opert bought. Carl Liebich, an Opert customer and driver, remembers being roped in to help on these dock runs.

"I'd be at his shop and all of a sudden he would say, 'we're gunna make a dock run.' We'd all jump in a car with Jeannie, his secretary. We would stop at different dealerships on the way and we'd pick up a Mustang or something, and if you picked up one then you'd follow Jeannie. And she'd drop off somebody else until we had about six cars and we'd all end up at the docks. Then Jeannie would be first in line, and the dock worker would say, 'Okay, Jeannie, what you got?' and she'd say six cars or whatever. And he'd say, 'Well, we've got to check the trunks.' You'd open up the first trunk and there'd be auto parts in there, steering units or something. The worker would smile, raise his eyebrows and say, 'Oh Jeannie, what is this?' Then they'd close the trunk and they'd send the cars over. Fred never worried about this stuff or seemed concerned about anything."

After John Powell bought his Chevron from Opert he stayed at Opert's parents' rent-controlled apartment in the Bronx. This was where the mechanics stayed. Opert suggested to Powell that he could work for him, and in payment it wouldn't cost him anything to go on an upcoming Colombian trip. Powell tells the story of one of his jobs:

"Freddie would say, 'okay, we are shipping muscle cars to France. I want you go down to Jerome Avenue.' Jerome Avenue in the Bronx, back in the day, was the used car capital of the world. Freddie would give me ten bucks, in $10 bills, and he said, 'you're gunna pick this car up at this place, then you're going to stop on Jerome Avenue at the intersection of this street, and then you'll see guys walking up and down with a little toolbox on wheels. You wave at one and you give him the $10 and say, 'I want one digit changed. I want the first digit changed from whatever it is to one.' I famously remember picking up this white [Pontiac] 455 HO Trans AM, it had 60,000 miles on it. I dutifully flagged down the guy with the tool box, gave him ten bucks, and he dived under the dash, fiddling around, and suddenly it was 10,000 miles. I had to drive the car down to the docks where they'd load it up and ship it to France. It was a cult thing in France at that time to have an American muscle car."

Opert was a shrewd business operator, even to the point of not being willing to sell his employee, Rick Mansfield, a race car while he worked for him.

"He wanted me to work on Saturdays," Rick remembers. "I think the deal was, 'If I sell you a car you're going to be farting around with it all the time.'

"I'd turned 21 and I had a few dollars that my grandmother had left me, supposedly for college, and he wouldn't let me go racing: 'I'm not going to sell you a car.' I worked for him for maybe a year and a half, two years. I had a chance to go to work for British Motor Corporation, that was just down the street. And the minute I went to work for British Motor Corporation he called and said, 'I've got a great deal for you. I've got a Formula Vee and a trailer for *X* dollars.' I said, 'That's a change of tune.' He said, 'Oh yes, as soon as you aren't here you become a customer.'"

The hardcore business man in Opert meant that, although he made many friends, his deals could upset some people along the way. For example, to increase his margin on an imported race car and its spares, he would sometimes strip off a lot of the good stuff – even the original, correctly-sized wheels. Then he would sell the basic car before offering all the components that had come with the car at an extra cost. Not everyone was happy with this but for Opert, business was business.

By the mid-'60s Opert had a solid business selling racing cars, parts and accessories; it was time to add another venture to Fred Opert Racing. Opert had identified an opportunity – sell a racing car to a wealthy 'gentleman driver,' then offer a turnkey service that would allow the time-poor owner to simply arrive at the track and race his car. He would pay Opert to prepare the car, deliver it to the track, and have Opert's mechanics look after it.

FOUR 4

Opert Invents the Rent-A-Race-Drive Business

The '60s were simple times in motorsport. English racing car companies that would become big names in the years to come were fledgling organisations, working out of old factories or abandoned mills. A designer/builder might sketch his ideas in chalk on the concrete floor (although Brabham's early premises only had a dirt floor) then start welding steel tubes until he created the chassis he had in mind. Once a prototype was complete, it was off to the track to discover how it performed. If improvements were required the car was taken back to the factory, the welding torch was lit, and changes made. Once the car was declared satisfactory then the drawings could be created from which production models would be built.

Companies like Jack Brabham's Motor Racing Developments (MRD), Eric Broadley's Lola, Bruce McLaren's McLaren, Derek Bennett's Chevron, Colin Chapman's Lotus, and of course Cooper, were all producing race cars, often by trial and error, using groups of enthusiasts working around the clock to meet the deadline for the next race meeting. Computers, wind tunnels, and computer-aided design were still years away for most racing teams, although Frank Costin had tested his aerodynamic theories at Lotus as early as 1954.

Fred Opert saw the potential that these English race car builders offered as the USA introduced race categories for both sports cars and single-seater formula cars.

Fred Opert Racing went on, over the following two decades, to become the North American importer for a number of racing car marques, including Brabham, Chevron, Titan, Tui (Supernova), and Tiga. These covered numerous racing categories, such as Super Vee, Formula Ford, Formula B, Formula Atlantic, Formula Two, and sports cars. He also imported and sold parts, including Hewland transmissions, as well as dealing in secondhand race cars.

In addition to his agencies and car sales, over 15 years Opert ran cars for paying drivers, initially racing regularly himself. He opened a racing driver school; he set up and ran a Formula Two team to race in Europe; and, as well as the USA and Canada, he entered cars in events as far flung as New Zealand, Australia, Japan, Macau, Mexico, Colombia, Venezuela and Argentina.

Opert had a gift for building excellent relationships with people who were not known to be the easiest to deal with. Two such personalities key to Opert's business were Derek Bennett and Brian Hart. Bennett was the founder of the Chevron racing car company, and the design genius behind its success, while Brian Hart possessed similar talents in the realm of race engine development. Bennett was shy and quiet; Hart was prickly. Keke Rosberg describes the Opert/Hart relationship:

"Brian was a difficult man to have a good relationship with, but Fred did. Brian trusted him. I don't think he would have given engines, without payment, to anybody else in the world."

Fred Opert was the first to run a motorsport service business where a driver bought a car from him, then paid his company to prepare the car, take it to the track, work on it during the race meeting, then transport it to the next meeting. Opert primarily attracted well-heeled 'gentleman' drivers, plus some drivers who had secured sufficient sponsorship to cover the cost of his turnkey service. His ability to attract wealthy clients was impressive – many were the sons of well-to-do families.

Tom Davey knew Opert from 1966, when he bought a trailer from him. Ten years later Davey drove one of the first Tigas in the USA for Fred Opert Racing. He compared Opert to some of the sport's best known business personalities:

"Fred was not one of the guys. He was different, a bit like Bernie Ecclestone. He had his mind on different things. He had a vision of what he wanted to do, and he did it. Like being the first to use a tractor-trailer for transporting race cars. He envisioned himself like one of the European impresarios, as a Max Mosley or Bernie Ecclestone ... He always put the deals together. Fred was the first guy to capitalise on the rent-a-ride concept."

In addition to income from his drivers, Opert sought the support of advertisers/ sponsors. Opert became aware of the Valvoline Oil and Motor Lubricants Company in 1963 when he was working for Carl Haas. Valvoline stickers appeared on the sports cars Opert raced in 1965, and he talked about using Valvoline products in his race cars in an article that appeared in the *Valvoline World* magazine:

"Last year [1965] three of our Elvas were winners in class at the Grand Prix at Guadalajara, Mexico. Going there we took a big white five-gallon Valvoline can on the airplane with us. The woman at the customs booth in Mexico City didn't speak English and gave us quite a time – she thought we were smuggling something."

Opert purchased a trailer that carried six Formula B cars to transport his and his customers' cars to the tracks. He approached Leonel 'Len' Manley at Valvoline to sponsor this rig, which was known as Big Red. The two men became good friends. As well as having its advertising on Opert's cars, Valvoline also got involved in the stands that Opert had at motor shows, including New York and Chicago.

One of Opert's prospective customer-drivers was John Bisignano, best known later in his life as a motorsport commentator with ESPN. Bisignano was a racing driver in the '60s prior to becoming 'Supervisor – Sports Marketing – World Wide Motorsport' for Valvoline in the '70s through to the mid '80s, and – as a result – continuing his relationship with Opert.

"I know they bought him [Fred] some transporters. Again, Fred wheeled and dealed. I don't know how he went about it, but he got them to buy a bunch of equipment that he needed to move cars around. And I think he did a lot of things for them. At times, if somebody was bringing him money to run a car and they didn't necessarily need the space on the side of the car, he would apply the biggest Valvoline sticker he could. So, it was a quid pro quo.

"Certainly he was the guy back in the day. He was really big on presentation and that type of thing as well, which set the mark for a lot of other people ... He would never wrench himself, but he knew the kind of people that it took to turn a car out the right way and keep it running the right way. He gave a lot of guys, like Barry Green[1], real opportunities, but real responsibilities too, when they were young guys."

Long before joining Valvoline, Bisignano raced in England and mainland Europe in a Formula Ford with Frank Williams; he was Tony Trimmer's teammate. After that, Bisignano wanted to do Formula Three in Europe, but it was the last year of the 1000cc 'screamers' that had become prohibitively expensive to run.

"I was looking at North American racing. Fred was really the first entrant to have a 40-foot transporter with six Formula B cars inside. Formula B then was very much like a Formula Two car, basically the same chassis with just a de-tuned engine. In the States, that would have been the first professional series for me to step up to. And he [Fred] had done very well in the series with several cars, so I contacted him about coming on board, and I went to Upper Saddle River, New Jersey, from Colorado. And I'm fortunate, having been around Frank's [Williams] shop with Piers Courage's beautiful Formula One car sitting there. Fred's shop was A-plus for everything, not much less than Frank Williams in F1. So I knew I was in a place that had good organisation, good knowledge of the series, and the sport in general.

"Frank was a guy who could get the job done, and Fred Opert was a guy who could get the job done. Fred Opert could talk faster and smoother than Frank Williams. That actually put me off just a bit. Of course, I was worried about just being a customer driver and not getting all the attention that I had in a little two-car operation where I was pretty spoiled."

Bisignano considered the option of organising everything himself, getting an English mechanic, a camper van and a trailer. He figured that this would cost him about 70% of what he would have to pay Opert. In the end he chose to race in Formula 5000, which proved to be a mistake for his racing career:

---

1   Barry Green later became a successful IndyCar team owner, his KOOL Green team twice winning the Indy 500.

"... I didn't go to Fred Opert in the back of the transporter with the other guys, and 'go out there and show us what you got.' And that was a mistake. I should have done it.

"Fred could have made me a winner in Formula B, but there was no way I was going to make myself a winner in F5000. The F5000s and the Formula Bs were running at the same events, so all season long I got to see Fred's wonderful organisation doing extremely well."

As well as running cars for paying drivers, Opert was dealing in race cars; not only importing and selling new cars for various UK companies, but also dealing in secondhand racing cars.

Opert employee, Rick Mansfield, remembers the company's growth during the early days:

"It was an adventure and it just kept growing and growing. In the beginning amateur guys were in sports racing in Mk8 Elva Couriers or Lotus 23s, and he [Opert] would bring those in and he would put together a package for whoever bought them, that he would drag them up and down – mostly the east coast – for all the national races. That's where he built his clientele. Then he started to find a bunch of guys, actually from around the world, I think he had a Japanese kid and I think Héctor Rebaque, and a couple of other guys from Mexico. They were from wealthy families and he started dragging them around. It was probably the very early times of what you might call pro racing. They didn't speak any English, and I'd just send the bills to their fathers. I thought, 'that's a pretty good gig.'

"He'd do all of the races and these guys would fly in. None of them hung around. About the same time he started hiring a bunch of mechanics from New Zealand and Australia. I was a pretty good drinker, but once these guys showed up ..."

One of those New Zealanders was Dave McMillan, who met Opert in 1969. He went to England with Kiwi driver Graeme Lawrence, then went to Canada before calling Opert for a job and moving to the USA where he lived in an apartment in the Bronx owned by the Opert family.

"Fred was pretty damn good fun. He had good customers, but he didn't have good mechanics, then us Kiwis turned up, and later Barry Green. We probably got Fred better organised. We worked hard but that is what we were used to. The Americans went home at five o'clock!

"Fred was very good at looking after us. We probably weren't even legal to work in the US. The customer drivers were very good too, often paying for our meals. The English hadn't appreciated us. The Americans did."

Opert was known for always having a smile on his face and rarely getting rattled, but McMillan remembers a couple of occasions when the American lost his smile:

"I went to Japan with Fred on two occasions. We took three cars the first time. The cars had to be drained of fuel of course. One of the mechanics forgot to reconnect a fuel line and the plane was turned around because the crew smelt fuel. Fred wasn't happy about that.

"Fred had a small shop with a yard. We put the cars out the front each day and had to put them back at night. It was sometimes a tight fit. Anyway, one night, for a bit of fun, we stacked the single-seaters on their sides. Fred wasn't pleased!"

As well as being a top mechanic and race engineer McMillan was a very successful racing driver. He was the New Zealand Gold Star Champion in 1976/77, 1978/79 and 1979/80 and the winner of the New Zealand Grand Prix in 1981. In 1982 he won the American CASC North American Formula Atlantic Championship. He raced occasionally for Opert.

"I never paid a dime to race. Once Fred said, 'Why don't you race at Saint Louis?' I took a Titan, put it on pole and won the race, and Fred sold five cars after that."

McMillan went on to join Opert's Canadian ex-partner, Brian Robertson, who established RALT America. He worked for Robertson for almost 20 years.

Opert was passionate about English race cars and their creators. Despite not being an agent for Lotus, he was moved to write a cheeky letter to the doyen of English motorsport magazines, *Motorsport*, questioning why Colin Chapman had not been recognised with one of that country's honours. His letter was published in May 1967.

> Sir,
>
> Here in the United States we do not pretend to understand your honours system. In fact, we hadn't heard of it until you knighted the Beatles! However, as a member of the large United States automotive scene I can't understand how Colin Chapman of Lotus has failed to be rewarded for his amazing contribution to your export prestige over here, when Jim Clark and Jack Brabham have come home with pieces of parchment or whatever they get. Is it because Chapman hit a cop? Jim Clark hit a Dutch cop much harder two years earlier.
>
> If my memory serves me right, in 1965 Colin Chapman, who could have hired one of several drivers as good as Clark, won just about everything that could be won in single-seater racing. World Championship, Tasman Series, F2 and F3, plus Indianapolis, especially Indianapolis which had never ever been touched before by a British car and yet his car won it, completely changed the design thinking of the United States racing world, and gave more of a boost to British automotive exports in one day than all the Prince Phillip visits and British ballyhoo put together. Does Chapman have to lay his cloak

in a puddle in front of Queen Elizabeth to get knighted or
should he get himself a guitar and sing us a few pop songs?
Paramus, New Jersey. Fred Opert

It's unlikely that Opert's letter had any influence, but Chapman did receive a
Commander of the Order of the British Empire (CBE) three years later for his services
to exports.

Having secured the import/distribution rights for Brabham racing cars in 1966,
1967 saw three Opert drivers as contenders in the SCCA Formula B Northeast
Division: Fred Ashplant, Joe Grimaldi and Mike Hiss, running Brabham BT21s.
George Wintersteen missed the early races, but when he joined the Championship
with another Brabham BT21 he took the title. Ashplant finished third and Grimaldi
fourth. Opert also flew in the future Formula One driver Peter Gethin for the St-
Jovite Grand Prix at Mont-Tremblant, where the Englishman took pole position
but failed to finish. The success of the Brabham drivers undoubtedly brought more
business Opert's way.

The championship results for the 1968 SCCA Formula B Northeast Division
reflected Opert's success as the local Brabham importer. Of the 21 drivers who scored
points in the championship, 11 of them drove Brabhams.

Rich Jacksic, who joined Opert in the late '60s, remembers the size of the Fred
Opert Racing operation at that time. Joe Grimaldi looked after sales, Tom Pomeroy
was running the shop. Then there was Timmy from England, Herb Schnider, and
Gerry 'racer' Walsh (whose wife was the secretary when Jacksic first worked there),
and there were guys in the parts department.

"That was on Route 4 in Paramus, New Jersey. We outgrew that place pretty
quickly. At the time we were doing Brabham, Chevron, Titans, Alexis, Hawke. We
moved to a bigger shop in Upper Saddle River. We had two parts guys, two
secretaries, I was running the shop by then. We had six, maybe seven guys working.
We had a Formula Atlantic team, a Super Vee team, a Formula Ford team, and on
any given weekend all three teams would be out racing.

"People thought that Fred was sponsoring people. Fred has never sponsored
anybody; other than Keke [Rosberg], everyone was paying - everyone. That was our
business, that was what we did. We rented cars, but we basically prepared people's
cars, transported them and provided track support. At the time we had five cars in
the tractor trailer, and we had a three-car open rig, and a two-car open rig. Don
Parker trailers from England. We sent guys all over the place.

"Barry Green was there, Bernie Ferri, Keith 'Wombat' Devereux from Australia,
Ross Sale I think, Smithy [Bill Smith] of course – he was a fixture – and there was a
gopher or two. But keep in mind also that it was seasonal, a lot of the guys from

New Zealand and Australia would go home in the USA winter. There wasn't much to do until the formula races started rolling around again."

1969 was also a special year for Opert in the SCCA Formula B Northeast Division, both personally and for business. Opert won the championship driving a Brabham BT21 for most of the season, then a BT29. Opert Brabhams took five of the first eight places, while two Opert-imported Chevrons B15Bs were sixth and seventh on the championship table – all this in the year that he got married to Sharon 'Sherri' Scheibelhut.

Even though the provision of a turnkey service to paying drivers was Opert's main racing business in the '60s and early '70s, as early as 1969 he was running professional drivers under his team banner. The 1969 Continental Championship finished at Sebring two days after Christmas. Fred Opert Racing took the first two positions on the podium, with Swede Reine Wisell in a Chevron beating Australian Tim Schenken in a Brabham. Both professional drivers had flown from England for the race, which was something of a continuation of their season-long European F3 battle that had even included a dead heat finish. Third place was taken by Brian Robertson, entered by Fred Opert Racing Canada. Opert was still driving in those days and finished 11th in a Brabham BT29.

The Reine Wisell entry came about because Opert was an agent for both Brabham and Chevron (an arrangement that would later cause him considerable angst). Schenken (the Brabham works driver), Robertson and Opert were all entered in Brabhams at Sebring, so Chevron scurried around to get their works driver, Reine Wisell, a Chevron B15B. Their efforts paid dividends when Wisell saw off the Brabham BT29s.

In his interview with David Gordon in 1989, Opert recalled the lead up to the race:

"I remember Schenken and Tony Trimmer and Reine Wisell and David Wilson [of Chevron], all arrived for our Christmas party (the race was on the 27th). They arrived at ten [pm] and we picked them up, and they went straight into our Christmas party, which was in full swing. We had a big party that year with a black rock and roll band, and Reine and David just arrived and David fell asleep in the middle of the party. He was sleeping in a corner and they hung all sorts of signs on him and took pictures.

"I think what happened was, somehow I invited Schenken to drive a new Brabham there [at Sebring] and when David Wilson heard that Schenken was coming in a Brabham, that meant all the Chevron guys would get blown off, or he figured they would. He wasn't going to let that happen so he says, 'Will you supply a Brian Hart motor?', or whatever we were using [Vegantune], 'and we'll send Reine Wisell and a car and I'll come over.' I think my mechanics probably took care of it. And I said, 'Sure, no sweat.' So the two of them were there, it

24

Continued on page 33

An Elva Courier on Opert's stand at the New York Auto Show. (Courtesy Fred Schuchard)

A Fred Opert Racing advertisement in Formula Magazine in 1971. (Courtesy Formula Magazine)

An Elva Courier on Opert's stand at the Chicago Auto Show.
(Courtesy Roger Dunbar Collection)

Mid '60s shot of a young Fred Opert, on the right, with a Formula C car he had just delivered to its new owner. (Courtesy Opert family)

Opert, his brother, Larry, in a Formula Ford, and Opert's wife, Sherri, 1970. (Courtesy Opert family)

Nick Craw, Jack Brabham, a happy Fred Opert, and Fumio Nagasaki in '72 at Suzuka, Japan. (Courtesy Hodgkinson collection)

Kiwi driver and mechanic Dave McMillan back in New Zealand for the 1978 NZ Grand Prix. (Courtesy Ross Cammick)

1 Marco Tolama in the Copa Novedades in Mexico. Note the Chris Amon-style helmet – Tolama's hero. (Courtesy Marco Tolama)

2 Bobby Brown, Opert and Nick Craw in Japan in '72. (Courtesy Hodgkinson collection)

3 Marco Tolama test session at the Autódromo Hermanos Rodríguez, prior to the Mexico City race, '79. (Courtesy Marco Tolama)

A corny Valvoline promotional photo with Opert, in the back middle, and Marco Tolama's car. (Courtesy Valvoline)

Opert with the ever-popular Linda Vaughn and Marco Tolama. (Courtesy Opert family)

was a great race, and Reine beat Tim – Tim in the Brabham and Reine in the Chevron."

1970 saw Fred Opert Racing gain even more success. In the 1970 SCCA Continental Championship for Formula B cars, Opert entries Eyerly, Lader and Craw took first, second and fourth places, respectively. Mike Eyerly, driving for Opert in a Chevron B17B, won eight times and came second on three occasions in a dominant display that easily secured him the championship for the second year running. Allan Lader drove a Brabham BT29, while Nick Craw campaigned a similar car. Evan Noyes bought a BT29 from Opert and ran under the Fred Opert Racing banner, he was second in the 1970 SCCA Central Division Formula B championship and was the Formula B class runner-up at the 1970 American Road Race of Champions.

But it was Eyerly who Opert rated as the best driver who ever drove for him:

"Eyerly was probably, as a talent, the best driver I ever had. I'd say better than any of the Formula One boys, I'd say better than Keke. I was still driving actively. That was the last year I really drove a lot. I had an exact same car as Eyerly, but he was two seconds a lap quicker than me; he was fantastic. It was maybe easier to appreciate him when I was driving the same car. You become a little distant when you become a team manager because you can't really feel what the car's doing. But as far as talent, watching him from the track and watching on the track, and being around him, and his attitude, I'd say he was definitely equal to any of the Europeans."

Sadly, after dominating Formula B and winning two championships in 1969 and 1970 Eyerly decided he wanted to do his own thing and left to race an uncompetitive Surtees Formula 5000. Opert was bitterly disappointed, as he believed that he could have taken Eyerly to Europe where he would have been successful in Formula Two. Instead, Eyerly's career faded and he was never able to show his class against European drivers, who Opert clearly thought he could challenge.

As an indication of how well Opert's racing business was doing in 1970, there were seven Brabhams and two Chevrons in the top ten championship places.

1970 was the year that Opert started to reassess the practicality of continuing to race himself, while also trying to manage his business and look after his paying drivers at the track.

"Through '70 I drove myself and was team manager, which was a very difficult situation because we had five cars and each guy had his own problems. There'd be one hour between qualifying sessions and this guy [wants] this and that, or 'your mechanic didn't do this', and 'I've got a shake in the left front.' And here I'm trying to drive myself, and as the team got bigger I couldn't really concentrate on myself."

In 1971 Fred Opert Racing was thriving with six entries at some of the SCCA Continental Championship Formula B races. The Opert camp must have seemed like the United Nations of motor racing at times, with drivers from the USA, New

Zealand, Mexico and Japan, in addition to mechanics from Australia, Sweden, USA, New Zealand and England.

In the championship, Kiwi Bert Hawthorne missed the first race and retired from the second in Monterey, but from then on he fought a great battle for the title with Allan Lader.

Hawthorne was an unusual Fred Opert Racing entry, as he was not driving an Opert-imported car. He drove a car called a Tui (named after a New Zealand bird). Its creator, Allan McCall, had modified one of his Formula Three chassis to suit Formula B.

In the end Allan Lader denied Fred Opert Racing its second championship, but the next three drivers were all Opert's – New Zealander Hawthorne, the American Craw, and van Beuren from Mexico. Craw was always in the top six, with his best result being a second at Road America at the end of the season.

Craw was heavily committed in his career running the Peace Corps; paying Opert to prepare and run his race car was the only way he could go racing. The demands of business meant that he needed to be able to just turn up at the track and know that he could slide into a well-prepared car. He didn't have the time to find his own mechanic, track down parts, and oversee the preparation and shipping of his car.

Although Freddy van Beuren raced a Chevron B18, Brabhams were still the mainstay of Opert's Formula B business, with Craw and Raúl Pérez Gama racing Brabham BT35s and Yoneyama and Junco in Brabham BT29s. Around this time Carl Liebich joined Opert's paying drivers with the Chevron he had bought from Opert the previous year. He summed up what it was like to be part of the Fred Opert Racing team:

"He was such a character. You almost forgot you were paying him!"

1972 was both hectic and successful for Opert. In the summer of that year he hired Linda Graham, who went on to become his longest serving employee. Graham joined the company in Industrial Avenue, Upper Saddle River, to look after the finances and accounts.

"I went to the interview. You know about Fred and women. He dated 'dipsos,' but he didn't surround himself with women who were stupid. I was tall, blonde hair, big blue eyes and had a pretty good brain. I walked into the interview and the first thing he said was, 'I'm buying race cars in England. Can you convert this from pounds to dollars and tell me how much I owe?' Well maths was always my thing so I blurted out the answer immediately and he said, 'Okay, you're hired!'

"He had race teams all over the place. It was my job to keep track of the money and make sure that everyone had what they needed.

"I am one of the most organised people, so he met his match with me. He trusted me implicitly. I probably signed more cheques as Fred Opert than Fred ever did. I took care of all his money and we never had an issue. It worked out very well for both of us. He was a hard task master and he was difficult to get along with for other people, but we never had an issue. One time he did raise his voice and I said, 'you'll never do that again to me,' and he never did, and we were good with that."

Graham and Opert successfully sorted out a sound working relationship as she went on to work for him for the next 28 years. In the later years she did his work on a part-time basis from her home as his business activities had decreased considerably.

Opert's house was often home to team members and the social hub for employees and drivers alike. This included younger family members, including Graham's six-year-old daughter, Alison. Graham remembers:

"Fred was big backgammon person, he loved backgammon. I said, 'You know Alison is really, really good at this.' Fred said, 'There is no way a kid could beat an adult at this game.' So we were at Fred's house. All the crew was there, the mechanics and everybody, we were like a family. Fred said something about playing backgammon and Alison looks at me, pleading, 'no, mom.' I said, 'Honey, what have you got to lose? If you lose you're a kid, if you win well ...' Anyway, she beat him. Six-year-old Alison kicked his ass and he never got over that."

In '72 Opert took on another distributorship, this one for Allan McCall's[2] Tui Formula Super Vee race cars. Nick Phillips of *Motorsport* magazine described how it happened:

"The Tui AM1 was a big success in Formula B, winning three of its five races and leading the other two. Soon McCall was designing another car for 1972. Initially schemed out as a Formula Atlantic (the successor to Formula B), bizarrely it first competed in Formula Super Vee.

"McCall and Hawthorne had reached a deal with Leda Cars to productionise the Tui, the idea being to sell a stack of Formula Atlantics to the US, via agent Fred Opert. He [Opert] also sold Chevrons though, and decided not to take the Tui Atlantics. What he did need was a Super Vee to sell.

"'Bert [Hawthorne] was still running Fred's driving school for him at Bridgehampton. He told a little porky, saying we had a Super Vee,' explains McCall. 'In just over a week, we took the first completed Atlantic car and converted it.'

"Hawthorne drove the Tui Super Vee in an international race at Daytona, finishing second to Helmüt Königg and ahead of Jochen Mass. That was really the last that McCall and Hawthorne had to do with the Super Vee; Leda built plenty, Opert sold them, and they proved very successful."

---

2   Allan McCall was a New Zealander. He had been Jim Clark's mechanic and had worked for McLaren. His close friend, Bert Hawthorne, drove for him and was involved in the Tui car development and funding. McCall died in New Zealand in 2017.

Opert's racing business included running sports cars as well as formula cars, and in February of 1972 the awkwardly named 'Doug Shierson[3]/Fred Opert Mexican-American Racing Team' entered two Ford-powered Chevron B19s for the Daytona Six Hours, a round of the World Sportscar Championship of Makes, for three of his regular paying single-seater drivers. There was one car for Nick Craw and Bill Barber, with the other for Mexicans Freddy van Beuren Jnr and Rudolf Junco.

In March, Fred Opert Racing ran Ford-powered Chevron B19s for the 12 Hours of Sebring, another a round of the World Sportscar Championship of Makes. Mexicans Freddy van Beuren Jnr and Rudolf Junco retired with an oil leak after 76 laps. Nick Craw and Bill Barber were more successful, finishing second in their class.

One of Opert's more interesting customers in 1972 was William Munstedt who bought a Lola T70 coupé sports racing car. Linda Graham tells the story:

"One day I had this young kid come in to buy a race car. He walked in the office and he had a bag full of money. People didn't usually pay in cash, but he wanted to for the deposit. So he sat down, decided what he wanted and ordered everything for the car. When he came back he paid for the car ... more cash. Sometime after that I had two men walk in, very official looking, and they said they were from the FBI and showed me their badges. They asked if I could tell them about this particular transaction. I looked back in the books and told them. It turns out that this kid robbed a bank to finance his race car and career. But they had figured that out and arrested him. They told me the trial was going to be in Brooklyn, in a month's time, and they wanted me to testify. I wasn't keen, but they said if I didn't go they would come and get me. So I went ... He was this squirrely looking little guy ... but he'd robbed a bank."

Opert had to give the money back and retrieve the Lola from the police compound.

It was in 1973 that two Australians, Barry Green and Bernie Ferri, joined Fred Opert Racing. Opert had gone to England to headhunt Ferri, who was working at Surtees. Ferri told Opert that if he wanted him he would have to take Barry Green as well, which he did.

After working for Opert, Barry Green went on to be a successful IndyCar team owner. His Team KOOL Green won the Indy 500 and the CART PPG IndyCar series. Barry Green remembers Opert's skills in attracting both good people to work for him and drivers who would pay to race.

"He was a good bloke. He was great for a lot of average drivers who had money to spend ... He was an important part of road racing in the US I think; and played an important part in a few drivers' careers."

---

3   Doug Shierson was a team owner who competed against Fred Opert in the '70s before moving into IndyCar in 1982 and winning the Indy 500 with Arie Luyendyk in 1990. Shierson died in 2004 aged 62.

Opert also played an important part in Green's career and in his personal life. When Green joined Opert, Jeanne Wilson was Opert's secretary. She and Green subsequently married.

1972 was also the year that Chevron fell out with Opert over what it perceived as a conflict of interest, as he was the Brabham agent as well as the agent for Chevron, which revoked his agency. At the time Opert's best ally at Chevron, David Wilson, had moved to Group Racing Developments (GRD). What wasn't known at Chevron, though Opert did, was that Brabham was going to stop producing customer cars, which would have left Opert with Chevron as his only Formula Atlantic offering. Bernie Ecclestone had bought Brabham in '72 from Ron Tauranac, and he told Opert earlier in the year that he was only going to do one more year of customer cars.

Opert believed that the driver Brian Redman had influenced Chevron's decision to drop him. Redman had gone to the States to race Formula 5000, where he met and spent time with Jeff Freeman in Ohio. Freeman had helped Redman, and Opert believed that Redman went back to Chevron and suggested it would be better off with Freeman as its agent, as Opert was selling Brabhams as well as Chevrons.

Opert expressed his feelings about what happened:

"So I found out that this fellow [Freeman] was selling cars, and I remember he sold one to Chip Mead, I think, who was a friend of his from Ohio. I don't know who else he sold them to, but he obviously couldn't get the right engines to run in the car or anything. And this was like the plot of a bad book, because the same time that they took the agency away from me I signed Bertil Roos, who was a brilliant driver in Formula Atlantic; really fast.

"So what happened was, we won the Super Vee championship easily that year. He was a real talent, Bertil, and we ran a few races in Formula Atlantic. They had some big races like at the Watkins Glen Grand Prix and some others, and we had to run a Brabham BT40. So here I had Bertil Roos, I had a brilliant talent, and I was sending him out to win races in a car that I couldn't sell the following year. So it cost me a tremendous amount of money and it set Chevron back."

Roos won the Formula Atlantic race at Watkins Glen, entered in a new Brabham BT40 that was owned by one of Roos' students at the racing drivers' school. Because he had lost the Chevron agency Opert entered Roos in a GRD for Super Vee races; a deal that Dave Wilson organized.

"The year I didn't have the [Chevron] agency they never won a race, and suddenly by the end of the year I was the biggest dealer in single-seater cars and I had nothing to sell. That one year really hurt the development of my company. It was just a shame. It really made me quite sad that it had to happen."

With Dave Wilson at GRD, Opert had ventured into European Formula Two, giving Bertil Roos his F2 debut in a DART GRD 273 in July at Mantorp Park. However, the GRD was not as competitive as a Chevron; Opert believed that if he had started his

F2 campaign with Chevrons then it would have helped the factory to have Roos in one of their cars. At the time Chevron was running Peter Gethin on a limited budget.

October 1973 was the start of the oil crisis when the members of the Organization of the Petroleum Exporting Countries (OPEC) proclaimed an oil embargo. This crisis impacted motorsport in a number of countries, and saw the sales of race cars reduce dramatically in the following couple of years, but Opert remained optimistic about North American racing.

Chevron was one of the companies hit hard by the oil crisis. In early 1974 Chevron had to lay off staff. The company was facing a serious situation that threatened its survival. When Opert ally Dave Wilson re-joined Chevron from GRD he convinced them to re-engage Opert, who then ordered six B27 cars to help them through their cash predicament. Opert didn't believe that the oil crisis would bite USA racing as hard as other parts of the world, so he took a chance and bought the cars.

Opert remained bitter about losing the Chevron agency for '73. He believed that decision had opened the door for Doug Shierson to capture a good slice of the market for March, for which he was the agent. But Opert can't have held a grudge against Redman as he took him to New Zealand in 1976 and he had a very high opinion of him as a driver:

"Redman was very fast, very dedicated, very smart. Never did anything stupid, knew how to win races... He wasn't just a good distance driver, he could drive anything."

Tim Coleman bought the Chevron company in 1983 and has the company's old accounting ledgers; they confirm that Opert and Count Rudy Van der Straten (Team VDS) were key to the company's survival. In 1974 Van der Straten ordered two B28 F5000 cars and paid for them in advance. He also paid his team's prize money into Chevron's bank account.

Jim Crawley was one of the USA-based drivers who drove for Opert from '74 to '76. Crawley initially raced a Titan Formula Ford after qualifying at Opert's racing driver school, where he later became an instructor. Crawley quickly moved up from Formula Ford to Formula Atlantic, racing an ex-Bertil Roos Chevron B27. He owned the car, which was prepared by Fred Opert Racing.

"Fred fielded some of the best cars on the grid. His crew prepared my car and Barry Green was my mechanic. Barry was a jewel of a man. The B27 was one of the most stable platforms that Chevron ever produced.

"Fred knew how to put a good team of people together. Professionally, Fred was strong and good. His track record speaks for itself. As a team manager he was very good."

Crawley had got to know Derek Bennett, the owner of Chevron, and when he was racing at Long Beach he gave Opert money to fly Bennett over from the UK to attend the race. However, Bennett didn't turn up as expected; Opert kept saying, 'He's been delayed.' After Crawley's race, Opert took him to the transporter and told him that Derek Bennett had been killed in a hang-gliding accident. Both men were shattered by the news.

But Opert and Crawley had a strained relationship.

"I was only 19 years old and had my own arrogance, and no doubt could be a bit of a smart-arse, which Fred didn't like, but I knew my cars and got results ... We also had a couple of social incidents, with a run in over a girl, for example. Fred never forgave me ... Then I got involved in exporting the muscle cars, but we were arguing about money all the time."

Their relationship ended in an irrevocable rift after Opert sold Crawley's cars and engines for him, but Crawley was not happy with the amount he received.

Throughout 1975 Opert continued to run cars in multiple categories depending upon the needs of his customers. One example was a one-off drive for IndyCar driver Gary Bettenhausen. A sponsor approached Opert to run a car for Bettenhausen at Trenton in New Jersey, and mechanic Duncan Pitcairn was given the job. He prepared a Tui Super Vee that was in stock and looked after both the car and the driver for the weekend, his only help coming from Allan McCall – the car's designer – who happened to be at Trenton that weekend with another car.

In 1976 Fred Opert Racing was regularly running cars for up to four drivers per race in the North American championships – CASC and IMSA. Eight different drivers were entered under the Fred Opert Racing banner, the regulars being Juan Cochesa, Hugh 'Wink' Bancroft and Gordon Smiley. There were a large number of Chevrons entered by other teams and privateers; presumably Opert had imported and sold the majority of these.

Such was Opert's reputation as a successful race car importer that when Tim Schenken and Howden Ganley started Tiga (pronounced 'tiger') and needed a North American agent, Schenken rang Opert in 1976 and declared: "You are going to be our first USA dealer." Opert agreed and ordered some cars. He asked Tom Davey to race the first car, who recalls:

"He owned the car and paid for the entries, and I had to get it to the track. He arranged a test and Tim Schenken came over to help sort it. I really wanted it to be good, but it was a squirmy little thing and Fred wouldn't put any money into developing it. They ran on radials in the UK but slicks over here. It just wanted to swap ends."

Despite this inauspicious start in the USA, Tiga went on to produce around 400 cars, enjoying success in many categories. The Tiga sports cars were particularly successful, winning championships and classes at Le Mans and Daytona. Although Opert was still officially a Tiga dealer until the early '80s, Schenken and Ganley appointed Michael Gue to take over the agency as Opert had stopped selling race cars.

As the '70s wore on Opert's business direction changed; he either wound back his USA based turnkey service to concentrate on running racing teams, primarily in Formula Two in Europe, or the business simply shrank due to his lack of attention to it.

For quite a while Opert had been the man in the racing service business, but others recognised his success and moved into the field, which consequently became more competitive. Rick Mansfield watched this happen.

"At some point, based on Freddie's success, other people started up; Joe Grimaldi opened up The Race Shop and two or three others opened up, all just in maybe 40 miles of where Opert started, doing much the same thing."

In 1978 Opert's North American operations involved both paying and professional drivers. While Fred Opert Racing ran a number of paying drivers during the season, Rosberg won three races for the team and he was occasionally joined on the grid by Swedish Marlboro driver Eje Elgh.

By 1979 Fred Opert Racing's activities in North America were a shadow of previous years, as Opert made the disastrous decision to join the ATS Formula One team as team manager. He did, however, run a car in all but one event for Marco Tolama, with a second car in a handful of races for Mark McCraig – a far cry from the years when the team had up to six entries for a Formula Atlantic meeting.

Tolama was a Mexican driver who had raced in his own country until 1977. He was looking for an opportunity to race outside Mexico when the Mexican newspaper *Novedades* organised a Formula Atlantic race in Mexico City called Copa *Novedades*. The newspaper's owner, Jose Antonio O'Farrill, came up with the idea for the event, which was facilitated by the fact that his father, Rómulo O'Farrill II, president of Grupo Novedades, was part of the group that brought Formula One to Mexico for the Mexican Grand Prix from 1962 to 1970.

Tolama saw this as an opportunity to race a Formula Atlantic car against some good competitors from invited American teams – Fred Opert Racing among them. He was aware that Opert had previously run a couple of Mexican drivers, including Héctor Rebaque, so Tolama contacted Opert through the organisers and an agreement was made for Opert to enter a car for him. This was the same race that Opert entered James Hunt, only to be thwarted at the last minute by Bernie Ecclestone. Hunt was, however, the Grand Marshall. With Hunt sidelined, Opert rushed in Bobby Rahal to take his place.

In an email to his nephew, Derek, Opert tells the story of James Hunt's escapades in this Mexican race:

"At the end of 1977 Elizabeth Butson [who looked after marketing for Phillip Morris in Latin America] arranged with Phillip Morris Europe, Phillip Morris Mexico, and the organizers of a late summer Formula Atlantic race in Mexico City, for sufficient start money to have James drive one of my Formula Atlantic cars in a race that slotted in during a two or three week gap in the Formula One schedule.

"James arrived on Sunday night, seven days before the race, and started partying immediately. Elizabeth dragged him out of bed each morning to do press conferences, radio, TV, and newspaper and magazine interviews.

"Bernie Ecclestone was not too happy about the reigning world champion driving in a Formula Atlantic race during the middle of the season. I was told he sent Herbie Blash to the FIA office in Paris to inspect the license the Mexico City people had for the race. It seems the license they applied for did not allow a Formula One driver to compete. On the Wednesday before the race we received a telex from Bernie Ecclestone stating that James should have a lot of fun and enjoy himself in Mexico, but if he drove in the race he should not bother to return to Europe for the remainder of the F1 season.

"I immediately called James in Mexico and explained the situation. He was not bothered as this would allow him to stay up even later with the two beauties that had moved into his room."

While James Hunt was enjoying the time with his Mexican lovers, Tolama had to take his racing more seriously:

"It was my debut in Formula Atlantic. People like Bobby Rahal came to race, and also some of the good drivers of that time in Formula Atlantic. I made good contacts. Then in '79, after I had a good sponsor who helped me to race in the 24 hours of Nürburgring, he [the sponsor] said that he wanted to help me."

Tolama had secured sponsorship from Herr Werner Will who owned Terramar, a charter plane company that brought German tourists to Mexico.

"So I saw that opportunity for 1979 to drive in the North American FA [Formula Atlantic] Championship, and I contacted Fred. It was not a very easy time because Fred was going to work for the F1 ATS team of Günter Schmid with Hans Stuck as the driver, so he told me, 'Marco, I want to run you in my team, but I have this [commitment], but let me see what I can do, and we will make this happen.' He liked me, and he thought I could do a good job with his team. He organised the team with one Canadian and two English engineers, and we did it."

Opert proposed to Tolama that he drive the Chevron B39 – despite being a 1977 model – because it was the same car raced by Rosberg, so the team had all the settings and gear ratios for each of the tracks. He also suggested to Tolama that he would buy a March or a Ralt ready for mid-season if that's what he and his sponsor wanted.

Opert bought a March in England, fitted one of his engines and had Swiss driver Mark Surer set up the car. Opert would attend the tests at Goodwood on his days off from his ATS F1 management duties. He was pleased with the March.

Tolama remembers his arrangements with Opert slightly differently, and was not enamoured with the March when he drove it:

"Unfortunately, Fred was working in Europe and we were doing the best we could in America. It wasn't that bad, because he was with us at Long Beach and with us at Halifax in Nova Scotia and at one race where we had a very peculiar weekend at Road America.

"We took the delivery of the March in the middle of the year, so at Road America we had the Chevrons (B39 and B45) and the March. But the March was no good. We had two cars there that had belonged to Keke Rosberg who was then driving Can-Am [The Canadian-American Challenge Cup]. He was there. I practiced the March, but it was no good because the chassis was twisting and, in the corners, was lifting the wheels. I said, 'This is no good. It is not drivable,' so we moved to the Chevrons again.

"That weekend there were people from England, people from Chevron, so they were very attentive to what was going on with me because mine was the only Chevron. I qualified around 15th or 16th out of 27 cars. But on my way to the grid the fuel pump on my car gave up, so I had to run to the other car.

"The second car they gave me [B39] was the car that had Keke Rosberg's set-up. Keke had a very particular way of driving. I am sure he could slide a car with downforce because he had a spectacular way of driving. Keke came to me on the grid to say, 'be careful, because the wing angle is different from the other car, so be careful.' Then he gave me advice, he said, 'At the carousel, jump a gear. Don't go from second to third, go from second to fourth, because in the middle of the corner the car understeers, because it is pushing with the power. So if you don't have that, you can exit the car very fast and you can go up the back straight faster than some others.'

"I did what he said, and it was really good because I started at the back of the grid and finished 12th. That was a good weekend."

Tolama has high praise for Mike Giddens, the English mechanic who looked after him. He found it amusing that Giddens would refer to Opert as "Fearless Freddie ... because he is fearless of any man, woman or beast."

Despite Opert's European commitments, Tolama was very happy with his year racing under the Opert banner. Opert's experience and coaching helped him, as did Opert's relationship with people like Keke Rosberg, Alan Jones, Derek Daly and Eje Elgh, who could all offer advice.

"I believe that this is the advantage you have with Fred. He was not your everyday team manager. First of all, he was a racer at heart, and he liked drivers who were racers; who would give everything on the track on race day. So I would say it was a great experience to work with him ... He was not one who would take your money and not give you value for it. He would make the best effort to keep you satisfied with what you were getting.

"That happened when I was running for him in '79. We had our big truck with the two cars and three mechanics. He liked to have them all beautiful, with nice uniforms. He loved his brand, he loved his sign with the helmet and the goggles. He was very proud of his racing team. He worked really hard to make it a force in racing."

The 'sign' that Tolama refers to is the Fred Opert Racing logo, a blue and gold depiction of a driver's face with an open-face helmet and goggles. Pete McCarthy who worked for Opert in '71 and '72 believes that the image is of American driver and constructor Jim Hall, who raced F1 in the early '60s, but is perhaps best known for his own racing cars, especially the Chaparral. Opert's original logo was far less distinctive, being a simple chequer with the words Fred Opert Racing, white on black and black on white.

Tolama was the last of Opert's paying drivers in North America. He witnessed Opert's struggle managing the ATS Formula One team, and the impact that failure had on the normally ebullient Opert.

"My sponsor was happy with what he got for his money, but then at the end of the year everything fell apart and we couldn't go ahead with what we had planned. I don't know what happened, but I think he [Opert] wasn't very happy with the way things went [at ATS], so I think he lost some of his motivation with racing. And he was never going to be the same, which is a pity as he was a man with a lot of energy."

The demise of Chevron, following Derek Bennett's death in March 1978, and the lack of competitiveness of the aging B45 were instrumental in Opert finally moving out of the racing service business.

Rosberg's B45 Formula Atlantic car was left at the Chevron factory, where it was seen by the talented but impecunious Jim Crawford after he returned from working in Switzerland. Author David Gordon reported that when Opert visited the factory Crawford offered him "a shoebox full of Swiss francs" for the car, which Opert accepted.

In an ironic twist, Opert purchased a March 79B from the man who had punched him on the nose: Joe Grimaldi. He entered this car for Derek Daly (at Trois-Rivières) and Eje Elgh (at Montreal). But even Daly and Elgh couldn't get the Opert entries to the front end of the field, so 1979 failed to deliver any success.

Opert's long-time sponsor, Valvoline, had continued to support him, and the huge Valvoline truck and trailer still appear in photos from that year.

A March 80A was entered by Opert for the first race of 1980 at Long Beach for Danny Sullivan, but the records show that he didn't even complete a lap after an altercation with rising star Jacques Villeneuve.

A car was entered for Westwood at the start of June, but it failed to arrive. That was the last time that the Opert name appeared on a list of entrants. Fred Opert, who had invented the rent-a-race-drive business, had closed the doors of his racing operation. It was the end of an era. It would return only briefly – and disastrously – in 1983.

Indianapolis 500 winner and team owner Bobby Rahal best summed up Fred Opert's impact on motorsport in North America:

"Fred helped build motor racing in the USA and Canada. He made his mark, and it was a big mark."

FI
VE
5

The Canadian Business and Trois-Rivières – a Little Slice of France in North America

Although smaller than the USA, the Canadian market for formula cars was strong. The Canadians had good tracks, close ties with England, and didn't have the Indy Roadster and NASCAR categories that were in place and popular in the USA.

Opert recognised that the Canadian Formula B category was growing and popular. By the third year of the series, 1969, there were 11 races across the country. This offered Opert a business opportunity, so in 1969 he joined up with Canadian Brian Robertson in a partnership called Fred Opert Racing Canada. From '69 through to '77 this business imported, sold, prepared and maintained Brabham and Chevron racing cars. It imported its cars directly into Montreal.

Robertson was in the banking business when he first met Opert, as a prospective customer for a racing car. He initially considered the racing car business as a sideline, but then couldn't see himself spending the next 30 years doing much the same thing as he had been doing already in banking, and so the racing business offered an opportunity for a more interesting career. Robertson was a championship-winning driver, and his success helped sell the company's cars.

Robertson was held in high regard by his and Opert's customers. John Powell, who was a paying driver, summed up his thoughts on the relationship between the partners: "Opert was a real deal maker. Freddie made the deals and Brian Robertson delivered on those deals."

In the 1971 Canadian Player's Formula B series Brian Robertson came second in his Brabham BT35, after a win and two second places in the six-race series. For the Mosport Park race in September more Opert drivers joined the fun, and four Opert entries finished in the first six places: Bill Brack came second, Freddy van Beuren third, Raúl Pérez Gama fifth, and Robertson sixth.

In a boost for the Chevron component of Opert's business, Brian Robertson won the 1972 Player's Challenge Series and the Canadian Championship in a Chevron B20. Fred Opert Racing also ran cars for four other paying drivers.

Having been a banker, Robertson and Opert were very different personalities, but despite this they enjoyed a successful partnership for eight years.

"I think we were relatively different people, but I would go stay at Fred's house. Sometimes we would go out together in London. But I remember one time we were at some pub and Lord Hesketh was there. Hesketh was going somewhere for a party and Fred was with him like a shot, and next thing I'm sitting there by myself!"

After he won the Canadian Championship, Robertson received a call from Opert telling him that he had secured Marlboro money to send him to Asia to race. That was when Robertson came to experience Opert's entrepreneurial approach to inexpensive flying.

"I'd won the Canadian Championship and Fred said, 'You need to go to the airport 'cause we've got some races organised for you for Marlboro.' It was the middle of winter and there was an ice storm. When I finally got to the airport in Ottawa I looked at the ticket and it read: Ottawa, Toronto, Chicago ... it just kept going. But it finally got me to Malaysia."

There were races in Malaysia, Singapore and Japan, but sadly the trip to Asia ended Robertson's racing career. Robertson crashed heavily in Singapore and suffered vertigo as a result. He'd destroyed his race car, but Opert shipped another for the Japanese race. Robertson's symptoms had eased before that race, but returned a few laps before the chequered flag. He managed to finish second but upon his return to Canada he lost his racing licence on medical grounds. Many years later he was inducted into the Canadian Motorsport Hall of Fame.

Robertson also travelled with Opert to Europe and never ceased to be amazed at the lengths Opert would go to save money on flights and freight.

"In those days, a lot of the airline tickets were hand written. He'd go to these bucket shops [airline ticket consolidators] in Britain and buy these cheap tickets. We'd go to the airport, sit down and look up at the monitor for the flight we wanted, then we'd get these little stickers and put them on the ticket, like it was supplied by the airline people, and fill out the flight, as though we were on it. Then he'd get on the phone, make the reservation, walk up to the counter, and fly. I'd never be up to doing anything like that, but to him it was just natural.

"A typical weekend with Fred is, 'we're going to fly to London.' The first thing you'd do is you'd get to the airport and you'd realise he's got 20 racing tyres and all kinds of stuff. And he gets there and he's bribing the Red Cap, and pretty soon the Red Cap gets nervous because he's taken so many tyres, and he has to go to get his boss. For a bigger bribe the whole mess goes. Then you'd arrive in Heathrow and somehow he'd get it all through customs. And on the way back we're taking Cosworth bits and giving them to the hostesses to put on the aeroplane in return for bottles of perfume. That was Fred."

Robertson discovered that Opert's network extended to enterprising ex-employees, as well as current employees, of the airlines.

"When I bought my Chevron he introduced me to a guy called Brad Chaffer and he says, 'Go with Brad to Pan Am.' So when I get to Pan American it's chaos, there's every kind of vehicle, from a bicycle up, and all these people with paperwork screaming at the clerks. Brad just walks by all this mess and everyone says, 'How you doing, Brad?' So anyway, I paid the bill and I'm flying this car on its feet for two hundred bucks. You cannot fly a race car on its feet. Normally you have to break it down and box it for that kind of money, but because Brad was an employee he got like a 90% discount. The fact of the matter is, Brad had flown over 20 cars that month, and he hadn't worked for Pan Am for nine years! He was a friend of Fred's. I don't know, maybe Fred was giving him something, I have no idea."

Formula Atlantic was adopted by the Canadians in 1974. The SCCA followed suit in 1975, using the Atlantic rules but retaining the Formula B name. These changes had no impact on Opert's business, as the chassis were the same but Cosworth-designed Ford BDA engines were now permitted. The Canadian business actually improved at that time, and Robertson set up a new facility in Carlton Place Ontario, where he installed a dynamometer that he purchased from Brian Hart.

Despite the oil crisis the Canadian Formula Atlantic series attracted big fields and provided good racing in '74. Fred Opert Racing had between two and five entries at each race, and Hugh 'Wink' Bancroft finished fourth in the series, consistently finishing in the top six. Roos finished a disappointing fifth. Both he and Howdy Holmes were the next most successful of Opert's drivers, with a number of second places between them.

Opert was disappointed with the mistakes Roos made during the Canadian Atlantic series.

"Here's my synopsis of the season – Bertil led every single race of the year and yet he never won one, and his car never broke. He led every race, never had mechanical failure, and didn't win ... Two of them that he won, he got penalized for yellow flag passing. The first one was a terrible thing to have happen, but the second one, there never should have been a second one. If you've got a big lead and you know that everyone's on your ass for passing on yellow flags, then you don't lap somebody on a yellow flag ... I couldn't do more. He had the two best mechanics, the best car, the best engine. It was capable of winning every race, and he was capable of winning every race, and he just blew every race. I think at that point we were probably out of money and Howdy [Holmes] wanted to drive a decent car so ...

"It was a very nice team with Bertil and Wink and Barry [Green], Bernie [Ferri] and myself. It was like a dream team, except that Bertil didn't win the races for us."

The records show that Roos didn't race at St Johns and Halifax, the last two rounds of the championship.

The '75 Canadian Formula Atlantic series wasn't a good one for Fred Opert Racing. The Chevron B29s were not in the fight for podium places until Trois-Rivières, where the Gitanes-sponsored French drivers Jarier, Jaussaud and Dolhem placed second through fourth behind Vittorio Brambilla in a Doug Shierson March 75B. Héctor Rebaque finished fifth in another Opert Chevron B29. It was Rebaque's best result for that year following an accident at Edmonton in the first round of the Canadian series.

When Rebaque first started racing with Opert he was just 16 years old. Even though he was a good driver, unlike other young drivers he wasn't particularly motivated; it was his father who wanted him to be a successful racing driver. He did, however, enjoy his time with Opert:

"I was very young at the time and we always had a great time. He was a very kind man, always laughing, making jokes with very good humour. I was 16 or 17 years old the first time I drove one of his cars. It was fun to be around him. That was Fred. He enjoyed the racing and he enjoyed after racing. You know what it's like with racing, there are always a lot of women around. We spent a lot of time, in Canada, in the United States and in Europe.

"The first F2 race I drove was at Estoril in Portugal and there was a very good party in Estoril after the race. I remember having a very good time. My father was always afraid that I was together with Fred you know, because I was very young."

Driving for Opert, Rebaque raced in Formula Atlantic and Formula Two in Europe. After leaving Opert he drove for Carl Haas before moving to Formula One in 1977, when his father paid for him to race a Hesketh. He subsequently raced several privately-owned F1 cars, competing in 58 F1 Championship races. He retired in 1983 after a year in Champ Cars, a very big accident, and a final fling in an F1 Brabham. He was still only 29 years old when he retired.

Perhaps the good times that he had in-between the races are what kept Rebaque motivated to do his best in the cars.

"There were two Venezuelan guys, Juan Cochesa was one of them. We enjoyed our time together a lot with Fred. Barry [Green] was our mechanic. These two guys were fun to have around. These guys were a lot older than me, 27 or 28, and of course Fred was older. We were always laughing. Fred used to call me 'the kid' all the time, and I say, 'don't call me "the kid", you're crazy.'"

Opert rated Rebaque highly:

"Héctor Rebaque, for his age, was fantastic. He was driving for me at 16 years old. At that point you had to be 21 to drive in America. This held back a lot of Americans. He, for his age, was brilliant, but he didn't want to be a race driver, he did it because his father wanted him to be a race driver."

New Zealander Tom Hooker, who was working for Opert at the time, remembers some of the fun the team members had on their Canadian travels.

"We were at Gimli – north of Winnipeg. The mosquitoes were as big as horses. We were at the track, which is an old airfield, and right there was a go-kart track, and the South Americans got their rental cars, took them on the go-kart track and they're having a great old time while the MPs [mounted police] are just standing there watching.

"Eventually, they walked over and stopped it, and suddenly those South Americans couldn't speak a word of English! The crew chief was summoned over, Smithy – he was a New Yorker, and even speaking English was a problem for him – but anyway he said, 'I'll translate.' Of course, he didn't have a clue what they were talking about, so he just made up stories.

"When we were in Nova Scotia, we were staying at this hotel and in the middle of the dining room was a huge tank with crayfish in it. They had rubber bands on their big pincers. But the South Americans got in there and they cut the rubber bands. At dinner they said, 'we want that crayfish there,' and when the guy went to put his hand in the crayfish tried to have a go at him."

That same year Duncan Pitcairn – a junior worker for Opert – was also involved in some high jinks at the Gimli track in Canada. It was race three of the series. Fred Opert Racing had run Juan Cochesa and Gordon Smiley. Mechanics from three of the teams – Opert, Shierson and Haas – noticed that there was a quarter-mile drag event the day after the race that was offering prize money. After the drivers and team owners headed home the mechanics got together; they prepared a Doug Shierson March to enter in the drag race, and won. They used their winnings for a big party at the next race meeting. The team owners were none the wiser.

In 1977 Opert added to his workload when he became a member of the Formula Atlantic Entrants Association, along with Ecurie Canada, Doug Shierson Racing, his ex-business partner – and now Ralt importer – Brian Robertson, Pierre Philips Racing, and Bill Brack. The group was formed to help to oversee the Canadian series which, in an unusual arrangement, was being run with a single engine supplier: Kris Harrison of Ecurie Canada.

For the 1977 Labatt's Canadian Formula Atlantic series Opert ran Keke Rosberg alongside Gregg Young and, for some of the early races, Francisco Romero (these last two were paying drivers). At the last round in Quebec, Patrick Depailler and Jacques Laffite joined Rosberg and Young. The two Frenchmen had driven for Opert at the preceding non-championship Trois-Rivières race. Gilles Villeneuve won the series, while Rosberg was fourth, with one win and two second places. This was the year that he was also racing F2 in Europe.

It was at Saint-Félicien in '77 that Opert entered Didier Pironi, alongside regulars Rosberg and Young. Pironi was José Dolhem's half-brother, which may be how he met Opert. Opert recalled first meeting Pironi in '76.

"José [Dolhem] was late to the circuit, as he often was in those days, so we asked Didier to set up the car, which he gladly did. I watched him closely. I instantly knew that he was a special talent. When José eventually turned up, he didn't manage to beat Didier's best time. I knew then that this kid was good."

A year later at Saint-Félicien, Pironi out-qualified Rosberg. He finished seventh after being hit with a 15-second penalty. Without the penalty he would have finished second behind Gilles Villeneuve. This was the first time that the Canadian and Frenchman had raced against each other. The rivalry that grew when they raced in F1 has been cited to have indirectly contributed to Villeneuve's death at Belgium in 1982, at which time the two men were teammates – but not friends – at Ferrari.

1977 saw Brian Robertson move out on his own. He and Opert had drifted apart while Opert was concentrating on running his Formula Two team. Robertson believed that Opert had become more focussed on being a racing entrepreneur. So he established a company to import Ralt cars from Ron Tauranac, who had previously been Jack Brabham's partner prior to Bernie Ecclestone buying Brabham (the BT prefix to the Brabham model numbers was derived from 'Brabham Tauranac'). This would prove to be a smart choice by Robertson, as Ralt and March became the cars to beat in the late '70s and early '80s. Robertson was now operating alone and realised that to have a viable business he needed the USA market, and operating from Canada was not practical, so he moved to California.

Had he been so inclined Opert could possibly have become the Ralt importer, but his priorities lay elsewhere and Tauranac didn't like the margins that Opert was looking for on his cars.

The Ralts proved to be very competitive and became the race car to have. Robertson recounted a small incident that occurred a few years later that highlighted the difference in his and Opert's personalities.

"I think Fred thought I took it too seriously because once he came up to me at Long Beach and said, 'You know you oughta smile more. You've got the best car.'"

No doubt Opert had his usual big grin when he said this.

Trois-Rivières

While Fred Opert Racing entries were a fixture in the Canadian Formula B and Atlantic series, the Trois-Rivières races – held in the city of that name in Quebec, Canada – were special ones for Opert. Between 1973 and 1977 he entered 11 drivers who became successful in Formula One, including two future world champions, plus a two-time winner of the Le Mans 24-hour race.

The Trois-Rivières event was held in the warmth of August. The prize money was good, and the race attracted many entries from Europe, including Formula One drivers. Naturally French drivers were a particularly good drawcard, many of whom were entered by Opert along with sponsorship from the French Gitanes cigarette company.

'Le Petit Monaco d'Amérique,' as it is sometimes called (even though it is in Canada) attracted the best teams and drivers who, in the mid-1970s, battled each other in closely-matched cars. Rising stars like Gilles Villeneuve and Keke Rosberg were keen to take on established Formula One drivers in equal machinery. Formula Atlantic winners at Trois-Rivières include: Villeneuve (father and son), Michael Andretti, Roberto Moreno, Alex Tagliani, and Patrick Carpentier.

The first Opert entries for the Grand Prix de Trois-Rivières were in '71 and '72, when Brian Robertson came second in a Brabham BT35, then the following year he was again on the podium with a third place in a Chevron B27.

Opert was married at that time, and his wife Sherri remembers Trois-Rivières as a beautiful place that was so different and very French, even though it is located just over the border from Maine. Perhaps it was Opert's love of France that made this little slice of that country, so close to home, a special place for him to visit.

Hugh 'Wink' Bancroft, a regular Opert driver in the mid-'70s, also loved Trois-Rivières:

"... it was an incredible track, a street circuit that required tremendous concentration. It was very difficult to pass there. I really enjoyed it. Pau was the one track that was scarier than Trois-Rivières. It had off-camber corners and it was hard to get the car stabilised. Trois-Rivières was very European. It was a special place."

Opert started his string of French entries in 1973 with Jean-Pierre Jaussaud. That race was still being run for Formula B cars with 1600cc Ford Twin-cam engines. Opert entered French drivers for the next five years.

Jaussaud was joined by two other Opert entries for the 1974 race – Tom Pryce and Hugh 'Wink' Bancroft. Jaussaud had a much better result than the previous year, finishing second in a Chevron B27 behind Tom Klauser and ahead of Patrick Depailler. Bancroft finished 13th, and Pryce (who went on to drive in F1 for Shadow, and was killed in a freak accident at Kyalami when a marshal ran across the track) retired his Gitanes-sponsored Chevron due to an accident. All three Opert entries were Chevron B27s.

Opert and Jaussaud must have developed a good relationship over the previous two years, as the Frenchman returned in 1975 joined by his countryman Jean-Pierre Jarier; their Chevron B29s looked spectacular in their Gitanes cigarette livery, which Opert had gone to great lengths to ensure was perfect. Opert had two other entries for his paying drivers, Frenchman José Dolhem and Mexican Héctor Rebaque. Dolhem later had a brief Formula One career with Surtees; he failed to qualify twice and was withdrawn from his final race after his teammate was killed.

Even though none of the Opert drivers won the 1975 Grand Prix de Trois-Rivières, they did take the next four places. Jarier was second followed by Jaussaud, Dolhem, and Rebaque. This was an impressive result in a field that included Rahal, Villeneuve, Depailler, Walker, Gloy, and Brack.

When asked about his ability to attract a big sponsor like Gitanes, Opert pointed to the quality of his cars and the team's commitment to impressive presentation.

"They knew they were good cars, well-maintained, attractive cars. It wasn't like getting into some of the other teams where they would give you a dog. They weren't guaranteed to win or anything, but they were at least good cars and they were attractive to the sponsor … Quebec was very pro-France, they still are, and the Trois-Rivières section of Quebec is very French. They wanted French drivers, I think the first time I brought a French driver over the organizers got me Gitanes [as a sponsor]."

In 1976, and for the third year in a row, an Opert driver was on the second step of the podium. To the delight of the partisan crowd, Canadian Gilles Villeneuve won the race with future world champion Alan Jones second in an Opert-entered Gitanes-sponsored Chevron B34. They were followed by Hunt, Brambilla, Rahal, Tambay (in an Opert Gitanes B34), Gloy, Cobb, and Rebaque. Opert's other entries didn't fare well.

Opert told the story of a hair-raising trip to the airport after the 1976 event. Future world champion Alan Jones was on a tight schedule and in danger of missing his flight. Jones accepted a lift in Opert's rental car with José Dolhem driving. With time running out to make the flight, Dolhem put his foot down.

"Alan shit himself," Opert said. "I saw them off [at the airport], started up the auto, drove out the airport, put my foot on the brakes and nothing! No brakes! José had worn them completely out on the journey to the airport."

Jones has never forgotten the experience.

"I'll never forget it. I don't know what Fred had said to him [Dolhem], but it took me almost till I got back to London to get over it. I was shitting myself. He was on the footpath, going around the wrong side of trams and buses. He was as mad as a cut brown snake. He was like Villeneuve … he was never going to die in bed."

Jones was right about Dolhem not dying in bed, he died while flying a light aircraft in 1988. His half-brother, Didier Pironi, had died eight months earlier during a powerboat race.

With Keke Rosberg in his 1977 line-up Opert would have been optimistic about finally taking a win at Trois-Rivières, but his hopes were dashed when Rosberg crashed his Chevron B39 on the first lap. Depailler was the most successful of the Opert entries in third place. Jacques Laffite finished sixth and Gregg Young had an accident on lap 48.

Perhaps Opert's attention had switched to his European Formula Two team, even though his Trois-Rivières entries for '78 and '79 were name drivers: Arturo Merzario, Riccardo Patrese and Derek Daly. All three failed to finish, and sadly Opert's Trois-Rivières adventures faded out, just as his Canadian business had.

Married to Motor Racing

Before any race, a driver normally clears their mind of everything other than the upcoming challenge. But at Colorado in June 1969, as he was about to climb into his Brabham BT21 Formula B car, Fred Opert did have a distraction. There had been talk with his girlfriend, Sharon 'Sherri' Scheibelhut, about getting married. With his trademark smile, Fred told Sherri that he would marry her if he won the race.

His mind might have been full of questions as he prepared to ease himself into his race car. He enjoyed his racing, he had a growing auto business specialising in racing cars and performance road cars, and he had established Fred Opert Racing, the commercial racing enterprise that would become successful and famous across the world. Where was marriage going to fit into the life of a driven entrepreneur who was always on the move; always doing the next deal?

Opert had an eye for a good-looking young woman, so when as a college student Sherri was working in a curio shop next to Fred Opert's auto business in Paramus, New Jersey, during the summer of '67, he made his move.

"Fred came into the shop and that's how I met him. I think he might have seen me out in the parking lot or something, but he came into the shop. I think I was a sophomore in college. I went back to school and he stayed in touch with me."

Sharon found Fred's smile and warmth attractive, and their relationship developed over two years. She was also from a family with a love of motor cars, so she shared some of Opert's passion.

"My first major toy was a go-kart that my father built for me. We always loved cars. My father loved cars; he was a car buff. With Fred I always had a fun car to drive: a 912 Porsche, 914, 1600 BMW, 1800 BMW, 2002tii that was on the cover of *Car & Driver*. There was always a fun car for me to drive, a Ford Escort twin-cam BDA right-hand drive. But I couldn't leave anything in the car, a bag or earrings, because he would sell it in short order."

Sharon continued her studies for a chemistry major while working during her holidays. That work led to modelling assignments for the Bergdorf Goodman department store.

"The following summer, between my junior and senior year, I took a job at Bergdorf Goodman in the designer department. Bergdorf Goodman is a very pretty store in New York City, in Manhattan. They had a couturier department, and that was on the second floor and I worked there. One day someone came in and said, 'can you put this dress on?' and I did, and then I did some modelling in New York that summer. So that's how that happened. I think at one point I was on the cover of some magazine and Fred was on the cover of some other magazine and it was all terribly dashing."

During her senior year Sharon attended the occasional motor race, like Sebring and Daytona, when she could get away from school.

After she graduated she accompanied Opert to an SCCA Formula A/B race at Continental Divide in Colorado, which is where he made his promise to marry her if he did well.

"I'm not sure he won, but he married me anyway. I used to be in the pit with my stopwatches and, you know, worried. I always wore blue and yellow because of his racing colours, and I was tall and skinny and wore mini-skirts.

"Fred had a friend out there and he married us. So, there you have it ... It was a whirlwind courtship and marriage."

The friend was Rabbi 'Buz' Bogage:

"I was his camp counsellor and 'village chief' at Camp Morgan in New Hampshire. My brother, J P Bo, of San Diego, went to school with him. We all lost contact with him when he went off to the University of Virginia.

"He had purchased a bottle of champagne, and we had drinks, and I took them to the airport and they flew to Europe. Fred left me his Pontiac Grand Prix for months and I drove it in Denver. He was a happy, good guy. He was a great 'car guy' ... and I loved cars ... actually, a fun guy."

Fred's sister Judi has the following recollection:

"The story I remember was that Fred and Sherri looked in the phone book to find a temple and saw one named Micah, then they learned that the Rabbi was an old friend from Worcester, Richard Bogage, so that became the 'divined' venue, so to speak. I think their 'wedding reception' might have been drinks at the Rabbi's house."

The Rabbi doesn't remember that Fred and Sherri had brought witnesses with them from the race track. Rich 'Rick' Jacksic and his wife Ruth had been at the Continental Divide race meeting – Jacksic was working for Opert – and the couple travelled with Opert and Sharon to the Rabbi's house and were the witnesses at the wedding. Jacksic recalls:

"The only two people who were at Fred's wedding were my wife and I. We were racing at Continental Divide – a horrifically bad weekend. One driver was killed, one crewman was killed, people were injured. My wife's a nurse ... she ended up in the ambulance going to Denver with the driver, who was dead on arrival. She wasn't hired to be there, but they just said, 'does anybody have any medical experience?' and she jumped in.

"So, Freddie and Sherri decided they were going to get married and Fred got a phone book and started going through, I guess, synagogues in Denver. Picks, calls ... turns out the guy was his camp counsellor in Massachusetts when he was a kid. So Ruth and I were the witnesses. We had a Pontiac with us that we weren't taking back, and he left it with the Rabbi to try to sell it. And it was at the Rabbi's house, just my wife and myself and Fred and Sherri."

In February of 1972, in an interview for *Competition Press & Autoweek*, Opert described how his wedding happened:

"I said we would get married if I did well in the next race. At the [Continental] Divide track I had qualified fourth in a field of 35. In the race I was running third. She was sure this would be the day. Then I rolled into the pits halfway through the race with problems. She was crying, figuring the marriage had gone down the tube. But it really didn't make any difference. I had made up my mind ... I didn't want to face a big wedding back home. I think I would have chickened out."

Of course, there was some upset that the couple decided to marry in such an unconventional way, but Opert was anything but conventional. Sharon knew that they had upset their families.

"Our families weren't happy that we married the way they did. We didn't want a really big thing. It was a choice. Like it wasn't as if we had a lot of time to get ready. 'If I win I'll marry you!'"

Sharon says that both families liked their respective son and daughter in-law, so harmony soon returned.

Opert's wedding was remarkably similar to that of a man he had great admiration and respect for: German racing driver, race team manager, public relations officer and innovator, Huschke von Hanstein. Opert and Sharon even named their German Shepherd dog Huschke after the man. Coincidentally, von Hanstein and his wife Ursula also married in secret at the Nürburgring, where the race promoter bought a justice of the peace back to their hotel on his Vespa scooter.

During the five years of their marriage the Operts enjoyed a special time mixing with interesting people. They were regulars at colourful parties in New York, attended by Andy Warhol and others of the glamour set. It was particularly exciting for Sharon, who was from a small town and had aspired to be a school teacher. She didn't have any of this type of life in her plans, but Opert was very cosmopolitan and knew many fascinating and famous people from around the globe.

"People from all over the world came to look at cars or visit – it was a whirlwind of a life. We lived in New York. He had an apartment in the Bronx. I got a job teaching in a little school down the street. Even though I was a chemistry major, I taught first grade in a fairly poor neighbourhood – 60 first graders in my class. Fred would be travelling a lot and he would be in and out, in and out. So we moved up to a really pretty town across the river from West Point in New York. We had an old house, over 200 years old. It was a stage coach stop on the old Albany Post Road. We always had a house full of people because he was always bringing the mechanics or the drivers or whoever was all part of the team. They would come to the house, and it wasn't that big a house, but we made room for everyone. I loved to cook. Fred was always so warm and so welcoming.

"I would cook, and I think I did their laundry, and if I was at the race I would always get food. I was just mindful – motor racing is very intense. I tried to be as helpful as I could. It was like a larger sense of family."

Although Opert loved to party neither he nor Sharon drank.

"He didn't drink, and I didn't drink either. It wasn't any kind of significant thing or statement, we just didn't. The driving thing and the drinking thing just didn't seem to go together. Though I remember James Hunt and Lord Hesketh, and they didn't ascribe to the same program. They thought a little differently!"

Fred's grandmother, 'Bubby,' was very fond of Sharon and they became close. One day the long-legged Sharon wore a mini skirt when she visited. She said, "Bubby, how do you like my mini skirt?" To which Bubby replied, "Well dear, I think you should give it back to Mini because it's too small for you."

"I'll never forget it because I was so proud of my Twiggy look. Fred would have a booth at the [New York] Auto Show and I'm sure I wore my mini skirt and go-go boots there."

Fred and Sharon's marriage lasted only five years.

"Motor racing was the love of his life ... He was devoted to racing and cars.

"I wanted the picket fence and the little kids at home. I wanted to have a family. Fred loved little kids ... but having his own ... it really didn't work. In retrospect it didn't really fit with his work. He had to travel so much. It didn't work for us to have a family, but I was still on that path. I really wanted to settle down and have a family. We parted broken-heartedly. I was offered a job with Union Carbide in Chicago. We separated and then the divorce was final."

Late in his life Fred caught up with Sharon again. There was a Porsche event at The Breakers in Palm Beach, and Sharon saw Fred there.

"I was happy to see him, and we had a lovely dinner and evening ... We were always very fond of each other ... just on different paths."

He had a home in Delray Beach, and he would call her when he was staying in Florida.

"When I was with him later in life we laughed because I never ended up having children. I ended up having a business career. So you just don't know how things are going to work out. I did see him a few times in 2015 and 2016. And the University of

Virginia had a Christmas party, and we went to that. He was very dear, very gallant, and somewhat apologetic about us not having children."

Fred Opert never remarried, but he always had an eye for attractive and intelligent women. He did have one other serious relationship, which Opert's finance manager Linda Graham recalls:

"Fred was kind of a loner. I guess he was a bit of a womaniser. But there was someone. She's the one who I think he regretted ... regretted that he'd let her go. But Fred was not the most faithful person. She was amazing. She was smart, she was gorgeous. She worked for Northwest Airlines. She was a flight attendant and she was also a nurse. She was one of the most amazing people, and I think that was his big regret, that she slipped through his fingers."

But Opert never wanted to commit to a long-term relationship. He was simply too busy with his auto and racing businesses. He was importing cars and he was exporting cars, he had a race school, he ran his race teams, he sold race cars and performance road cars, he imported and federalised grey market prestige cars, and then there was always the next deal.

But, despite his work, he did create his own family, which Sharon commented on:

"He was very fond of the little family he put together with Nikolai. He looked upon him as a son."

Sharon is referring to Nikolai Kozarowitzki, the son of the Finnish racing driver Mikko Kozarowitzki, who drove for Opert in the '70s.

Nikolai and Opert's nephew, Derek, also remember Opert as something of a playboy whose girlfriends came and went very quickly. He always had a non-threatening charm that women found attractive, even as he got older, which Nikolai remembers:

"Fred could convince women to let him take pictures of them with their tops down. He had a good way of talking to women. He was not a good-looking guy, but he was a playboy and he played up."

Opert's niece, Lauren, believed that his view of women was formed by the time he was at the University of Virginia and in the machismo world of motor racing.

"Fred was a creature of a different era. He's always had incredibly high standards for anyone in terms of looks, intellect, discipline, etc. He was always someone who had certain men's way of looking at the world. Freddie was such a bundle of contradictions. He had such a life in the New York metropolitan area during the era of feminism that he touched on culturally in so many ways, and yet politically those ideas didn't quite enter his bloodstream. And I think his ideas about gender were pretty much formed playing football and dating in central Massachusetts at his high school in the '50s; and going to the University of Virginia in the era that he did, when women were expected to be a certain way and men were expected to be a certain way.

"Racing was of course his central domain, which is a male-dominated field, and he liked his Studio 54 life of models and glamour. Which I think was also part of the allure of the racing subculture. But that doesn't mean that he wasn't interested in intelligence, because he was, and so he was impressed with women who held their own. It wasn't just that women were decorative, but it helped if they could also be. There were definitely added points for that.

"Freddie was as equally impressed that Brooke Shields went to Princetown as the fact that she was incredibly beautiful. That was an ideal for him. He respected achievement and pedigree, but if there was a set of legs to go with it, that wasn't ever going to be a detriment.

"He lived as a 25-year-old for multiple decades."

Opert would turn up at his niece's parties, even though he was 35 years older than her and her friends, but everyone Lauren introduced to Opert liked him.

Opert would use friends and employees as co-conspirators in his plans to attract women. Rick Mansfield found himself in this role on a number of occasions.

"He often used me as a foil. He'd have someone he wanted to take out and they had a friend and the only way they would come was if their friend came. So he'd say to me, 'Friday night, don't do anything, don't make any plans. So and so's coming up and she's bringing a friend.' Well, you know, the friends weren't beauty competition material. They weren't race queens by any stretch of the imagination. But a couple of times I actually stole one of his girlfriends and I'd say, 'You asked me to come along. Don't blame me.'

"He was quite a ladies' man. He would spend the last part of half a day, Thursday if he was going to a race on Friday, dialling every broad in the book to see if he couldn't convince someone to go to the race track with him."

Needless to say not all of Opert's conquest attempts were successful, and Mansfield remembers when Opert was upstaged by Kiwi ace, Chris Amon:

"He [Opert] was pretty unique. At Bridgehampton, one year during the Can-Am, he brought this gal out, and I don't think she was much interested in Fred. Late in the afternoon Fred's looking for her and she's sitting on the trailer with Chris Amon. I've never seen a sadder man in this life, and the girlfriend comes back, picks up her stuff and takes off with Chris Amon."

But just as he was in business, Opert was entrepreneurial in his love life, coming up with creative ways to meet women. If there was a good looking woman in a car behind him going into a toll booth, Opert would pay his toll and hers then try to get her to pull over on the side of the road so he could meet her.

Carl Liebich knew Opert from the time he bought a Chevron from him in 1971, before becoming part of his team. Carl's parents had a summer house near the Road America track, which is close to the beautiful Elkhart Lake in Wisconsin. They also had their home quite close by. They suggested that the team could use their summer house when they were racing there.

Opert "always had a stewardess or someone like that with him," Liebich remembers.

"Sunday morning we're at the track, Fred's not there yet, and my parents go to the summer home; they're going to clean it, because the guys had been there. And they walk in the house and they go into their bedroom and there's Fred with a stewardess in my parents' bedroom."

Opert's hairline was receding even in his 20s and he was prone to put on weight – his night-time raids of the refrigerator were legendary. Later in his life his friend Keke Rosberg would call him "the beaming egg," but women found his charismatic smile, love of fun and boundless energy attractive.

Motor Racing Schools

As Opert was the foremost importer and seller of formula cars in the USA, and had been instrumental in making formula car racing popular in North America, establishing a motor racing school made business sense. Not only was there money to be made running the school, but the graduating students were ready-made prospects for the sale of racing cars and associated services. So, Opert opened his first motor racing school in 1971 at the Bridgehampton race track in New York State.

Opert told Barry Sale, a New Zealander who was working for him at the time, about his plan.

"When I got back in the country in early 1970, Fred told me he wanted to start a Drivers' school at Bridgehampton, and to start writing the brochure, which I distributed at the New York Auto Show that year. The instructor the first year was Bert Hawthorne, and then Freddy van Beuren after Bert was killed.

"That was the same year that Alan McCall brought the Tui Formula B car over for Bert to drive. I handled the day-to-day running of the school, prepared the cars, and had a great time spending my weeks in the Hamptons and traveling to races on the weekends. After I left in early 1973, the school moved to Pocono [Raceway, Pennsylvania], as developers were making serious moves on the Bridgehampton property."

An advertisement for the school appeared in the *New York Magazine* on April 10th 1972.

On the Track

If you have a driver's licence, can drive a standard shift, and will spend $500 for a three-day education, you qualify for the Fred Opert Motor Racing School at Bridgehampton racetrack. Schoolmaster Opert, 32, has raced for seven years, was Northeast champion, in 1966 and 1969, and claims to be the world's largest racing car dealer. Instruction is held on Tuesdays, Wednesdays and Thursdays 9 to 5, April 18 through October. Head instructor, Bert Hawthorne, who just won the

Formula 2 race in Bogotá, takes you out first in a Dodge Colt
compact, to teach you the procedure for driving the course,
and you spend the rest of the time in Formula Ford racing
cars, working up to 120mph and an International Motorsport
Association professional licence so you can race at exalted
tracks like Lime Rock and Watkins Glen. The school provides
your suit, helmet and motel room; you supply the racing
shoes, socks and fireproof underwear. FRED OPERT MOTOR
RACING SCHOOL (201) 825-1151

The advertisement claims that Hawthorne had won the Formula Two race at
Bogotá, in Colombia, in February of that year in a Brabham BT38. The records from
that period record this as a Formula B race, but the categories were similar. A
Mexican driver, Freddy van Beuren, finished fourth. He was a friend of Hawthorne's
and in tragic circumstances he took over as the instructor at Opert's school when
Hawthorne was killed at Hockenheim on April 14 of that year.

Van Beuren had been racing for many years, and had bought a Chevron B18 from
Opert and raced as part of the Opert team – with Hawthorne and Nick Craw – in the
Formula B championship. He explains how he became Opert's instructor at
Bridgehampton:

"When Bert died Fred called me and he said, 'Freddy, would you like to drive a
Super Vee in races with me?' So I went. I got the job as an instructor. I had never
instructed. I had, like, an hour lesson from Fred and he said, 'this is what you have
to do.' We had a very good mechanic; a New Zealander, Barry Sale. He was the
mechanic in charge of the cars. So I went to become an instructor and it was a lot of
fun. We had a very, very good time and a successful year because there were lots of
students.

"We had six to eight students at a time. We had three Formula Ford race cars. We
really gave the guys a lot of driving time. They drove and drove and drove and drove.
The first half day was a bit of teaching and what you have to do etc, and then
showing them the track ... teaching them how to heel and toe, which at that time
you had to use, not like nowadays with the electric paddles in the steering wheel. It
was really, really fun. Classes were from Tuesday, Wednesday, Thursday ... three days'
classes, and I used to live at Fred's house. When we went to Bridgehampton we used
to stay at a hotel.

"That year I probably drove [raced] about 20 or 25 weekends. One of my students at
the school became a very good friend of mine and he sponsored me to drive other
cars, so it was really exciting. My wife wasn't too happy about it mind you. She
would visit sometimes, but we had the two children who were like two and four at
the time."

Van Beuren enjoyed his time as an instructor and racing Opert's Super Vee, but with his family in Mexico there was pressure to return home. His wife was probably also concerned that he might have been having too good a time, given Opert's reputation as a playboy. So when Opert moved the school to Pocono, he decided it was time to return to his family and business in Mexico.

Linda Graham, who looked after Opert's business finances, also helped out with the administration and dealing with the students at the school.

"We had all of these people who envisage themselves as F1 drivers, but of course when they go to the driving school they find out the truth. We had this one guy from a very prominent New York City family that has incredible amounts of money. He came in and said, 'I'm so and so' and we said, 'okay fine.' We were always very nice to everybody. But he was a jerk. He and his wife decided they were going to do the course. Anyway, he got so nervous on the last day that he actually skated into the wall. It was more than he could handle. We thought that was one of the funniest things that had ever happened because he was such a pompous ass."

John Bisignano tells the story of when he was commissioned by his sponsor L&M cigarettes to produce a road safety film for the armed forces, Opert let him use the Bridgehampton school for the filming. To demonstrate different handling characteristics he decided to film a formula car and a road car. There was a Formula Vee available at Bridgehampton and Opert had just been given a new Dodge Colt by Dodge to race in an SCCA Showroom Stock series. Bisignano was filmed driving both cars around courses laid out with safety cones. Towards the end of the session he wanted to film the Colt spinning; this proved to be difficult. In one final effort he threw the car around the cones at speed and pulled on the handbrake. Opert's new Colt promptly rolled five times.

"I had to call Fred and tell him that his free Dodge Colt was completely smashed. Basically the car was a piece of junk. I don't know how we got it onto a trailer. So he wasn't very happy with John Bisignano at that point."

So he could buy another Dodge Colt, Bisignano gave Opert the money he was paid to make the film, and some additional money that L&M came up with.

"Any way some time later I got a call from Fred, 'You're $35 short on the cost of a new Dodge Colt.' I said, 'what can you salvage from the one I wrecked?' and he said, 'the radio.' So I said, 'go sell the damn radio!' Everything was done on a handshake in those days."

The move to Pocono was forced on Opert by the uncertainty that surrounded the future of the Bridgehampton circuit. Very vocal neighbours, who objected to the noise from the circuit, were applying pressure for its closure. It seemed likely that its sale to developers was imminent.

Opert broke news of the move to van Beuren.

"He said, 'Okay, for next year we won't have Bridgehampton, but we will have Pocono and I want you to be the chief instructor.' But my family in Mexico said, 'No.' I wasn't a kid anymore and I loved my wife and my children, so I said, 'No Fred, I can't do it.' We had a restaurant business that we had to attend to. So I left the school. I did go back a couple of times. Fred would call me up, and I became the emergency teacher … you know, Fred being Fred."

After moving the school to Pocono in 1973 a simple text advertisement appeared in the June 1973 edition of *Popular Mechanics* magazine:

> **Driving at speed**
> Road racing is a skill learned under the watchful eyes of
> professional instructors – like those at Fred Opert's Racing
> School, now at Pocono Raceway where Fred is also starting
> police driver training and planning a '74 high-school Formula
> Vee interscholastic league. For more information write to him
> at Pocono International Raceway, Box 500, Mount Pocono, Pa.

There is no record of the plans for police driver training, or an interscholastic Formula Vee league, proceeding.

When Opert needed to replace van Beuren he turned to Swedish driver Bertil Roos, who he had 'discovered' through Swedish engine builder Bertil Sollenskog when Opert went to him to source Formula Super Vee engines. Roos became the instructor for the school at Pocono and raced for Opert. He eventually took over the school and ran it himself. He may have bought the business off Opert, or, as van Beuren puts it, they did some sort of a deal.

Roos was a very quick driver, with an ability to be competitive in any category of race car. Rich Jacksic remembers that he saw Roos in action for the first time at an IMSA Formula Ford race at Sebring.

"We had been in Venezuela. Smithy and I flew home, picked up the tractor trailer, drove back to Sebring, Florida and Fred shows up. Bert had died and he would have been in the car. It was the big money race for IMSA FF. There had to be 50 or 60 cars in the race. Sebring's a big track. And he [Opert] shows up with Bertil, and we didn't have a clue [who he was]. He was fast right off the bat and he'd never been in a Formula Ford, he had raced a Formula Vee. Half way through the race we were giving him signs to tell him to slow down because the second placed car was Héctor Rebaque and he wasn't even in sight. The rest of the field was so far back it was silly, and the problem was, we sold cars to these people. It's not good to beat the hell out of your customers, and we had to tell Bertil to slow down."

On another occasion Jacksic was at Mosport, where they had borrowed a Brabham BT40 for Roos to drive. Bertil liked the car to oversteer. Jacksic said everyone else hated oversteer, but not Bertil. He kept asking Jacksic to make changes to the car, as he wanted to see the rear tyre out of the corner of his eye to get it sideways. At Mosport Roos went out and started running away from the field. Once again Jacksic had to give him the slow down sign. Jacksic was keen to leave and get back home, so at the end of the race – which Roos won handily – while Roos was on the podium, Jacksic got in the car and took off down the pit lane to get it back in the trailer. At the end of the pit lane he braked but the pedal went right to the floor, so he zipped back out onto the track, turned the car around and brought it back, managing to slow it up with the small amount of braking that was left with the pedal pressed to the floor. When he took the nose off he found that the front reservoir was bone dry; the master cylinder had let go and dumped all the fluid out. When Bertil came back Jacksic asked him when he lost the brakes. "Oh, the third lap." He replied. Jacksic had a high opinion of Roos' ability.

"He was a hell of a driver. I just had to laugh. Other guys are out there and there are all the excuses in the world while he wins with no front brakes."

Although Rosberg is often cited as the only driver Opert sponsored, it appears that he did help Roos as well. In an interview with author David Gordon, Opert explained how Bertil Roos came to work and drive for him.

"I had a driving school, and so what I could do was I could pay a driver if he would teach at the school. That's how Bert Hawthorne came to me the year before. And when Bert was killed in '72 I needed a teacher for the school. He was killed about two months after Bogotá and suddenly I didn't have a driver for the school. I asked Freddy van Beuren, who was driving for me in '71 in our Chevrons. Freddy was very experienced and a very good personality, so I got Freddy to come up and teach the school. He was married with kids, he had a restaurant to run with his mother in Mexico City, but I was in the shit ... so Freddy came and ran the school for the rest of the year.

"I found Bertil Roos through a fellow in Stockholm by the name of Bertil Sollenskog, who made the best Super Vee engines. I wanted one of his engines for a race at Daytona Beach at the end of '72. I really wanted one 'cause we were building our own engines and we weren't that competitive. I'd gone to Hockenheim and Nürburgring and seen that this guy's engines were really good. He said, 'I won't sell you an engine, but I'll come over and bring one you can use, no charge, if you let me pick the driver.'

"The people that are most conscious about the quality of drivers are engine builders, because when you've got a quick driver and he comes off the last corner on[to] the straight 12 miles an hour quicker than everyone else, he's going to pass them down the straight, and the quick guy goes by and the other guy says, 'Holy shit! What kind of an engine's in that car?' And that's what sells engines ... quick drivers.

"I knew that if he wanted this guy to drive, his engine he had to be quick. I'd never heard of Bertil Roos, he'd driven some home-made terrible Super Vee and had never done anything. So I had a brand new Tui. I think it might have been a new car for him that was built with the Sollenskog engine, in fact his engines were called Bertils Motors. Bertil is a name in Swedish like Billy or something would be in America, a very common name.

"He brought the driver over, I met him, and I think he was second in the race, but did very, very well. I was very impressed. That was the end of '72. Early in '73, as I was fishing around for a permanent replacement for Bert Hawthorne, I was so impressed with him I said, 'Well, would you like to come over, teach the school? You can drive a Super Vee.' So he came over and he brought over two Swedish mechanics with him and they all lived out at Pocono and ran the school. The Super Vees were kept out at Pocono because the school mechanics and a couple of others ... oh, Barry Green and Bernie Ferri first came over to work on the Super Vees with Bertil Roos."

Finding Roos is another example of Opert's ability to recognise a talented driver early in his career.

Jim Crawley, who drove for Fred Opert Racing in the mid '70s and was an instructor at the school with Roos for a short time, remembers the relationship between Opert and Roos as fractious.

"Roos was an arrogant son of a bitch. He and Fred were like junk yard dogs gnawing at each other. But Roos was a good instructor and the school was making money so Fred left him alone."

Linda Graham likewise found Roos to be difficult.

"He was a little bit stand-offish. I thought he was a bit of a pain in the ass. He wasn't the most pleasant person. I don't know if he took advantage of Fred, but he wasn't one of the nicest people I ever met."

Roos ran the school until his death, five months before Opert died.

The Racer

Was Fred Opert a good racing driver? That depends on who you ask. Before the demands of his businesses required his full-time attention, Fred Opert raced with some success, including winning regional single-seater championships. He mostly drove cars he imported.

Opert's first taste of competition was in his Jaguar XK150S. After he had completed the SCCA drivers' school training he raced the car at sprint meetings and SCCA events, including at Webster and Lime Rock.

Opert competed in single-seater race cars in SCCA events from the mid '60s, often joined by his younger brother, Larry.

In 1966, having been a sales agent for the Elva Courier since '64, Opert raced one of the diminutive English sports cars with William McKemie and Terry Petmecky in the Daytona 24-hour race. In the same year McKemie and Opert competed in the 12 Hours of Sebring. The entrant was Carl Haas Automobiles.

In March 1966 *Valvoline World* magazine published an article titled, 'Speed Merchant – The pursuit of fun and profit has made a confirmed Valvoline exponent of busy Fred Opert.' This Valvoline promotion covered Opert's racing and that of the drivers who competed under his banner. Photos that accompanied the article show the Elva cars carrying small round Valvoline stickers. This was probably the start of Valvoline's long-term relationship with Opert.

In 1966 Opert won the first of two Northeast Division championship titles; this one for Formula A cars. A big slice of opportunism was involved in this championship win, as there were no other Formula A cars running in the Northeast Division. It seems that Opert had seen an opportunity and seized it: he realised that if he entered a Cosworth SCC-engined Formula C car, but with an engine capacity that exceeded the Formula C 1100cc limit, it would be categorised as a Formula A car (the SCC being a racing engine, and Formula B was only for production engines). As a result, Opert scored 18 points in the Formula A class, using a Formula Two Lotus 32, and won the championship.

Allen Brown, of oldracingcars.com, reported that Opert qualified for the runoffs, where he tried the same trick with a newer Brabham BT18, but for some reason he was disqualified. Brown thinks that perhaps the car was under the Formula A weight limit.

Brown noted that Opert tried the same ruse again in 1967, scoring nine points and tying for the title with Chuck Kirkbride's Lotus.

These championship titles might have been good for publicity purposes but can't have been very satisfying for Opert; however, he would be back in 1969 to win on his own merits.

In 1967 Opert visited the Chevron factory in Bolton, UK, and met Chevron owner Derek Bennett. He attended a test session for the new BMW-powered sports car at Oulton Park. The Chevron people had great expectations for their new sports car and wanted to enter it in long distance races, but there were problems getting an entry for Le Mans which left Daytona and Sebring as good options. Opert could see an opportunity to race a serious sports/racer and was impressed by the car. Chevron recognised he had the USA infrastructure it needed to support its entry in the USA races: Opert had trucks, mechanics, a workshop, Valvoline support, and was good at attracting sponsors. Opert recalls:

"It was ideal, because they really couldn't just fly it over, or boat it over, and then arrive at Newark or Jacksonville and get a rented truck and go to the track without any tools, or jacks, or fuel in cans, or all the other things you need. So I guess because I knew him [Derek Bennett] and was interested in his progress, and I had a viable racing team, it was natural for him to do it. Just like when we went to New Zealand, we went to people who we were friends in New Zealand to help us out a little bit."

So Fred Opert Racing entered Derek Bennett's development BMW-powered 2-litre Chevron for the Daytona 24-hour race, which gave Opert the opportunity to drive with Peter Gethin and Roy Pike. The car was later designated as B4, although Opert dubbed it 'The Valvoline Special' and it had sponsorship logos to match.

After engine problems leading up to the race – reportedly caused by Opert's mechanics' lack of experience with the dry-sumped BMW engine – Gethin and Pike were negative about the car and their chances. Pike, who was from California, had even booked an early flight that would leave five hours before the race was due to finish. Opert was upset by his co-drivers' negativity.

"To me it was a very exciting thing. It was the fastest car I'd ever driven at the time, but they just ... well it wasn't perfect next to a Carrera 6 or something like that, they were down on the project, negative the whole weekend, which to me was very depressing."

The car raced for six hours before it was retired. Reports from the race recorded that a rear wishbone broke, but Opert didn't recall that.

"There was some sort of a vibration or something in the car that I was happy to drive with, I guess. You know, I just wanted to drive. They [Gethin and Pike] felt it was dangerous. So they moaned to Derek that it was dangerous, and we were going too fast to take a chance. Probably they were right. I think Pike wanted it withdrawn so he could collect his pay check and be with his parents, or wherever he wanted to be, in California on his nine o'clock plane ... It raced but it was retired in the evening. As I said, I wanted to keep it out there, but I think due to enthusiasm and inexperience; whereas they were in the middle of what they thought were valuable racing careers, and they thought it was dangerous."

This event was significant in Opert's future motor racing business as it was his first association with Chevron.

For the '67 Sebring 12-hour race a Porsche 911S was entered by the Valvoline/Opert Racing Team. The all-USA driver line-up had John Pauley, Bill Bowman and Lee Cutler join Opert for a solid 15th place after starting 39th.

Joe Grimaldi, who had co-driven with Opert when he worked for him, had a low opinion of Opert's driving skills, and Tom Davey, who was both a customer and a driver of Opert's, shared Grimaldi's view: "Fred was a notorious terrible driver. The whole thing would have worked better if he didn't try to drive."

Rick Mansfield, who also worked for Opert, was similarly off-hand about Opert's driving skills: "He was a much better businessman than he was a driver. He had a tendency to get off quick as hell then drop a wheel off in the first turn."

But given Opert's later success, winning the SCCA Northeast Division Championship in 1969, he must have been more than competent. He raced a handful of Formula B races in Brabhams in '68, and a Porsche 911 in '69 for the Sebring 12-hour, Daytona, and the Wolverine Trans-Am race in Michigan.

1969 was Opert's most successful year racing in Formula B. He won the SCCA Northeast Division championship with 42 points, the highest score in any of the SCCA's seven divisions. Opert raced a Brabham BT21A for most of the season before switching to the new BT29 for the last races, by which time he already had a solid lead in the championship.

Opert also raced his Brabhams in some Continental Championship races including Sebring, where Fred Opert Racing entries appeared in numbers for the first time and took the first three places: Wisell, Schenken and Robertson.

Rich Jacksic's opinion of Opert's driving ability differs from that of Davey and Grimaldi.

"Actually, Fred was quite good you know. He was in Formula B at the time in his Brabham. He was probably second or third at the runoffs. He had a shunt in the first turn at Daytona and that put him out of the race, but he was very competitive in that. But now, in the pro series which eventually came up, he would not have been [competitive], not with Rahal, Rosberg and Howdy Holmes, you know all these characters, these guys were fast ... they were scary fast.

"He held the lap record at Lime Rock in an Elva Courier at one time."

Jacksic did wonder how Opert managed to race, as his hands always shook. He suffered tremors and later in his life people assumed that he had Parkinson's disease, but that was not the case.

"The funny thing was, one time, for Christmas, we bought Fred a calculator. A digital calculator, when they were not common. At the time it was $100 for this thing. It was a lot of money, we all had to chip in. But the problem was Fred's hands shook so bad he would hit two or three keys at the same time, so he had to use the pencil eraser, and I'd think, 'How the hell does he drive a race car when he can't hold his fingers steady?' But he was a pretty good driver."

For the 1970 USA Formula B season Opert raced a Chevron for the first time, a B17B with a Ford twin-cam engine. Opert rated this Chevron as his favourite of all the racing cars he drove. He also raced a Chevron B16 sports car in the Daytona 24-hour, but failed to finish.

It was surprising that Opert was able to race so often, as his team was running cars for runaway championship winner Mike Eyerly, as well as Nick Craw, future champion Allan Lader, and Evan Noyes. Eyerly, Lader and Craw were all very good racers, and Noyes was on his way up, so generally Opert's paying drivers crossed the finish line ahead of him, but he still finished consistently mid-field or better.

The Daytona NASCAR race is a huge event on the USA's racing calendar, and before the Daytona 500 NASCAR races there were Formula Ford races. Opert and his brother, Larry, competed in the IMSA Formula Ford race at Daytona in 1971. Although the races were for lower category Formula Ford cars, they attracted many drivers from higher racing categories because the prize money was significant. For example, Donnie or Bobby Allison, and other top NASCAR drivers who drove in the 500, also drove in the IMSA race. Several drivers from the Continental Formula B or Atlantic series, like Brian Robertson and other members of Opert's teams, competed as well.

By 1971 Opert was entering up to five cars a race in the Formula B series, as well as selling Brabhams and Chevrons and keeping an eye on his new motor racing school. It was no longer possible for him to be looking after his customers while racing as well, so his name disappeared from the Formula B entry lists as a driver.

One of Opert's last races was back at Daytona for the professional 1973 IMSA Formula Ford race, where the top three cars crossed the finish line together and the order was only determined by a photo. Opert was third. Fred's brother, Larry, thinks that Danny Sullivan finished a few inches ahead of him in second place. Fred and Larry had started across from each other on the grid.

Opert's final drive in a Formula Atlantic car was memorable, but for the wrong reasons. For the Grand Prix weekend at Watkins Glen in October '73 there was a support race for Formula Atlantic. Opert hadn't raced an Atlantic car for almost three years, but he decided enter for the Watkins Glen race. Rich Jacksic was working for Opert at the time and was none too happy with the debacle that ensued.

"Because it was the preliminary to the F1 race, everyone came out of the woodwork. Everyone wanted to get into an Atlantic car, because they all thought that Frank Williams or someone was going to see them and sign them up. You know, because 'this guy is so blindingly good we have to get him in an F1 car!' So there were a lot of rentals that weekend. I remember it was called the Colombo Yogurt Grand Prix, and I remember that because the truck was filled with Colombo Yogurt. I was eating that stuff until it was coming out of my ears. Anyway, Fred wrote the Brabham off in practice. He never made it to the race."

In yet another of his masterful deals Opert was responsible for Colombo Yogurt's sponsorship of the Grand Prix event.

Opert didn't go out on a high, but when he retired from racing he gave his race car number, 73, to his brother Larry. 73 had been Opert's uniform number when he played college football.

An American in Europe – Formula Two Team Management

Until the mid '70s Fred Opert Racing had primarily been operating a turnkey racing service business, although Opert would enter and provide cars for professional paid drivers, when deals could be put together. An early example of this was in 1973 when Opert entered Frenchman Jean-Pierre Jaussaud in the Canadian Trois-Rivières race in a Brabham BT40.

Perhaps the fun he had in New Zealand, and his team's success there in 1976, '77 and '78, caused Opert to shift his emphasis from his North American racing service business to running teams overseas, or perhaps the racing service business had just become too competitive in the USA, as others started similar businesses to get a share of his success. Even though he was used to juggling many balls at once, the travel required to run race teams overseas might have made it too difficult, even for Opert, to devote the time needed to his North America-based racing service. He may have got more of a kick out of putting deals together to run professional drivers than he did from his home-based turnkey business. He certainly enjoyed the glamour of the European F2 races and tracks. Although, in a 1978 interview in *The New York Times*, he stated that the primary reason he began running teams was to sell the race cars that he imported, it seems unlikely that running teams outside North America would increase sales of the cars he imported to the USA.

Initially, Fred Opert Racing team cars were shipped from the USA to whichever country had a race meeting Opert had entered. Later, when he was running Formula Two in Europe, the cars were based in the old cotton mill that had become the Chevron factory in Bolton, UK, where Opert rented space.

Opert put deals together to run his cars – product sponsorship, money from the promoters (Japan, New Zealand, Mexico, and Trois-Rivières, Canada), and in some cases drivers who still paid for their drives or brought sponsorship money with them. Nick Craw, who drove for Opert in both sports and formula car events, considered him to be a master at doing deals for sponsorship; attracting the funds needed to run his cars.

One constant Opert supporter was Valvoline. Opert also enjoyed a close relationship with Marlboro, and had a number of other non-automotive sponsors

over the years, including Gitanes cigarettes, *Newsweek* and Ramada Inns. But Julius
Schmid, the Durex Sheik condom manufacturer, was the one that raised some
eyebrows and led to some creative car presentation by the Opert mechanics; a
suitably erect condom appeared on the nose of Rosberg's pink Excita-sponsored car.
Some in motorsport's establishment in the '70s tut-tutted at sponsorship from a
condom manufacturer. Perhaps, as Sir Jackie Stewart put it, this was a time when
motor racing was dangerous, and sex was safe.

Linda Graham prepared the successful sponsorship proposal for Julius Schmid.
The whole team, including her, had smart pink shirts, jackets and caps.

When asked what his secret was, in being able to put together sponsorship deals
in Europe that were often better than those locals could manage, Opert replied:

"Usually I had good drivers, not always. I'd say 50 per cent of the time I had good
drivers, but when they were good they were very good drivers. And often, being a
strange American team, we could get more press. Like if we went over for three
races, everyone wanted to know why we were there, what we were doing, who's
Bertil Roos, or [Jean-Pierre] Jarier, or whoever we had in the car. And I think the fact
that we'd done so well in Formula Atlantic, and our cars looked good."

Opert's team was admired for the standard of presentation of its cars, and this
was something that Opert took great pride in. In 1978 he even had his favoured
sign writer from Paramus in New Jersey – known as 'Hank the Brush' – flown in
to England to paint the bodies of his cars at the Chevron factory, because he
didn't think anyone else could do it as well. Opert explained how this came
about:

"Now every team looks beautiful because it's so commercial, but at that time we'd
made a real outfit and the cars had to look good. In '78, when Philip Morris,
Marlboro, sponsored Eje Elgh in our car, [I had] all my cars in England. I didn't really
like the signwriters. I didn't think they were as good as the guy I had in America. So
I called up Hogan at Philip Morris, at Marlboro, and I said, 'What do you spend a
year for lettering and painting the McLarens?' For a two car team he said it's X
amount, so I said, 'Well, would you budget, I don't know what it was, $600 to do
Eje's car?' He said okay, so I got my local sign painter in the next town, Paramus –
his name was Hank the Brush – and I said, 'Hank, what are you doing next
weekend?' He said, 'I don't know.' I said, 'How would you like to come to England?'
So we got him a standby ticket, you could buy a ticket for England in those days for
$198 each way.

"So we flew him over Pan Am standby, [he went] up to Bolton and he painted all
our '78 cars. We did about three spare noses for each car and everything was done
really nice. Your average British team had stick-on numbers and white roundels.
White stick-ons! They looked awful on the car."

Opert brought a higher level of professionalism to top-level European racing.

Continued on page 81

Héctor Rebaque and fellow countryman Marco Tolama. (Courtesy Marco Tolama)

VALVOLINE-OPERT RACING TEAM

1 Tambay, Jones, a happy Opert and José Dolhem at Trois-Rivières in 1976. (Courtesy Lee Lobowski)

2 Sharon 'Sherri' Opert with their dogs, one named Huschke after Huschke von Hanstein. (Courtesy Opert family)

3 An early photo of Opert; his Brabham is sporting his original company logo. (Courtesy Opert family)

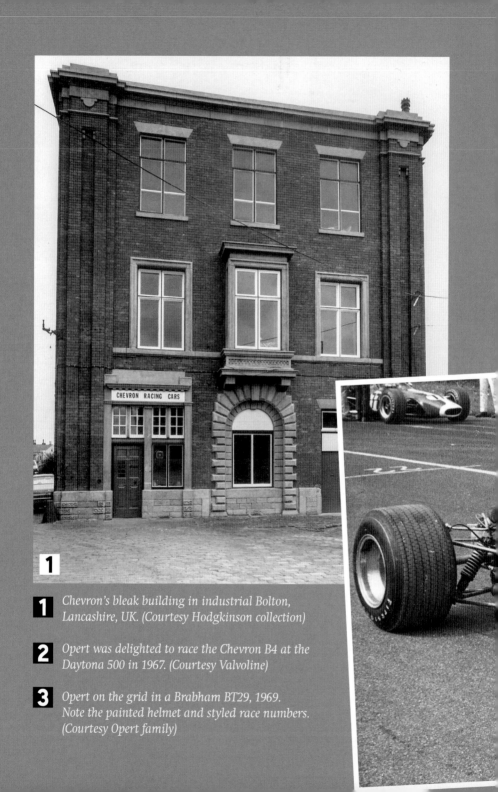

1 Chevron's bleak building in industrial Bolton, Lancashire, UK. (Courtesy Hodgkinson collection)

2 Opert was delighted to race the Chevron B4 at the Daytona 500 in 1967. (Courtesy Valvoline)

3 Opert on the grid in a Brabham BT29, 1969. Note the painted helmet and styled race numbers. (Courtesy Opert family)

2

3

1 *Brother-in-law Jim, brother Larry and Fred Opert. (Courtesy Opert family)*

2 *Opert enjoyed the world of F2 and his relationship with Gitanes. (Courtesy Opert family)*

3 *Bill Smith, Rosberg and Opert with the Excita condom-sponsored car. (Courtesy Marc Sproule)*

4 *Héctor Rabaque's Chevron B27 with Chevron Petroleum sponsorship in 1974. Note the USA signage on the trailer. (Courtesy Hodgkinson collection)*

Opert with the Valvoline Girls in Bogotá. (Courtesy Opert family)

*Bogotá winner Bobby Brown, the mayor of Bogotá looking concerned,
a happy Opert and a thirsty friend. (Courtesy Bobby Brown)*

"I was the one that instigated that you could have one number all year in Formula Two, 'cause it was like a club race thing, you'd go to Portugal and you got number 16, so you'd put a white sticker on and the cars looked like shit. And so I was the one who got a number for the whole year. The champion got number one and it went down from there. That way you could have a nice looking car. Also for the spectators and the journalists it was good. You knew that number 17 was Jacques Laffite or Héctor Rebaque or whoever it was. Also it was good for journalists because you could then fake pictures!"

The mechanical presentation of the cars matched the visual presentation. Opert had the same ability to attract good mechanics and team members as he had drivers. Neil Bailey, who worked for Chevron when Fred Opert Racing based its Formula Two team at the factory, did fabricating work for the team, and saw first-hand how it operated.

"From a race team point of view, you couldn't have got any better race mechanics anywhere else in the world. As pure race mechanics, and I've met a lot over the years, those guys were, for me, absolutely top-drawer. The thing is with Fred, he always seemed to be able to put a real good gang of people together. He just had that ability, and it was a pleasure working with them. Fred's team were a real good bunch of guys. You couldn't have wished for better."

Opert was confident of his ability to recognise good mechanics and employ them:

"I'm not a mechanic, but I can go to a race and watch a mechanic work for ten minutes and I can tell you if he's good or bad. I've always had the best mechanics, I had better mechanics than any Formula One team."

When Linda Graham joined Opert to look after the company's finances she quickly became aware of the high standards that Opert set.

"Fred was not easy, it had to be exactly the way he wanted it to be. You could eat off the floor in the shop, it was that clean. The guys wore white shop coats, and nobody could have dirt on their hands. The place was almost sterile. The guys worked really hard, but they were all interested in racing. They loved what they were doing, and they wanted to win too. They were the ones who were responsible, so when we won races it was a really big deal because they had won as well. They were an amazing group of guys."

Opert had his first foray into the European Formula Two Championship in 1973 after Dave Wilson, who had left Chevron, was working at Group Racing Developments and convinced him to bring Roos to Europe to race the GRD. The entry was under Dart Racing and Opert had sponsorship for two races. Roos drove extremely well, and, in the race at Mantorp Park, in his home country of Sweden, he led defending champion Mike Hailwood, in a works Surtees, for most of the race.

Opert enjoyed the world of Formula Two.

"It was just very glamorous to me and I liked that. I liked the places Formula Two raced and I liked the press. David [Wilson] got me to go the first time because David had seen what a good driver Bertil was. He [Wilson] had a very good driver killed earlier in the season and he didn't have a works driver. So when Roger [Williamson][1] died, David suddenly didn't have a star and he could see the star potential of Bertil Roos, which we both could. He worked out a very friendly deal with GRD that if we would bring them X amount of sponsorship Bertil could drive the two Swedish races. And Bertil managed to get the sponsorship himself."

In '74 Opert ran Bertil Roos in the first two F2 races of the season. Roos finished eighth at Montjuïc Park, Barcelona, and sixth at Hockenheim in Germany. These were Roos' last two Formula Two races. He subsequently had success in Super Vee and Formula Atlantic in North America. Photos of the Chevron B27 that Roos raced in Europe show a car almost devoid of advertising. *Motorsport* magazine archives describe Roos as a protégé of Opert, so perhaps Opert funded this short European venture, or Roos found the money. Unlike many of Opert's paying drivers, Roos was personally financially bereft.

Away from motor racing, Opert would have experienced some personal angst in 1974 as this was the year that he and Sharon divorced.

Things got serious in 1975 for Opert's team in Europe. Austrian Harald Ertl contested ten races for the team, with Mexican Héctor Rebaque racing in half that number. Two other drivers, Maxime Bochet and Jean-Pierre Jaussaud, did one race each. Frenchman Bochet only raced in his home event, the Pau Grand Prix, in a Chevron B29, where he failed to finish. That was his last single-seater race, but Opert – who was visiting Pau for the first time – was impressed with the Frenchman, with whom Opert had done a hire deal on Rebaque's Chevron B29.

"We had a French driver no-one ever heard of. He drove very, very well, but he punctured and bent a wheel, but he qualified very well and drove very well."

Frenchman José Dolhem (Didier Pironi's half-brother) and Harald Ertl were Opert's main drivers in the European Formula Two Championship of 1976. Dolhem contested eight races and Ertl six. Others who did more than one race included Hans Meier, Juan Cochesa, Jacques Laffite, and Jean-Pierre Jarier. There were single race entries for Rosberg, Howdy Holmes, Rupert Keegan, Jochen Mass, Rolf Stommelen, Tom Pryce, and Hans Binder. Ian Grob was an Opert entry in the Formula Libre Shellsport Group 8 European Championship for the last two rounds at Brands Hatch late in the year. Grob had raced in some earlier rounds without success. His switch to an Opert Chevron B35 with a Hart engine resulted in one seventh and a 14th place. Formula Libre included cars from a number of categories, including Formula One.

---

1   Roger Williamson, who was killed in an F1 car at Zandvoort, had been GRD's F2 driver.

Opert's deal with Harald Ertl was clever. Opert needed a car for Jacques Laffite – who was the reigning F2 champion – for three races, but it needed to be a BMW car, which was quite different from Opert's Hart-engined cars. Ertl was a journalist, short in stature with an impressive beard and a moustache that curled up at its ends. Opert entered Ertl, and helped him get the BMW engines that he could use for the year in exchange for use of Ertl's car for Laffite's three races. Because Opert had Gitanes sponsorship for Laffite, he arranged a spare body in Gitanes colours that they could fit to the car for Laffite's races. It was a happy arrangement for Ertl, Laffite, Gitanes, and Opert. Tom Pryce actually drove the car at Rouen instead of Laffite due to a conflicting commitment for the Frenchman.

Opert explained that he came to secure a Gitanes sponsorship deal for F2 races in France through the team's success for the cigarette company at Trois-Rivières in Canada.

"The effort for us in Atlantic, where we were the dominant team, to show up with our immaculate team and drivers like Tambay, Jarier, Laffite, Jean-Pierre Jaussaud, was compared to Ligier's team, which was always at that time at the back, and it wasn't a very attractive car. So when their [Gitanes] head marketing people came over from Paris to see the effort at Trois-Rivières, they were astounded by how beautiful the cars were.

"On a Gitanes packet there's a light Chartreuse green as well as the blue, so we had blue and green, and they said, 'Gee these guys can do the trick.' So when I went back to them – I also speak French – it took lots of trips to Paris, but I went back and I said we'd like to do the three Formula Two races in France, originally with Jacques, because he was their Formula One driver. So it meant that, beside every Grand Prix, at the three big French [F2] races they had a top driver and a top team and a great-looking car. Obviously, when Jacques came back to a Formula Two race, there was no way you couldn't have a picture of Jacques in a magazine. So it was a very good deal for them, and that's how we put it together."

Opert did get good support from Chevron for his F2 efforts, and his team was allowed to use the Chevron workshops in England. Opert had a small office there, his cars had their own space where the mechanics could work, and there was space for the trucks. This was the Opert team's home away from home, but because the team members didn't have homes and families in England they often didn't return to England if they were on the Continent. Opert described their options.

"Let's say there was a race at Pau and two weeks later at Rouen, all the English teams would go home, we might stay in France.

"We also stayed in Germany a lot. That was another thing Harald Ertl provided. His sponsor was near Hockenheim, he was the De Tomaso importer, and our mechanics used to use that shop. In fact, I would say the year Harald Ertl was there, the team was in Germany more than England 'cause we had maybe three or four races in Germany and it was easier. It was a long, expensive trip to go back and forth over the Channel and up to Bolton."

1977 was one of the hectic years when Opert was running his Formula Two team in Europe as well as Formula Atlantic in North America. New Zealander Dick Bennetts[2] was primarily responsible for the F2 operations. He was joined by the quiet Australian Bernie Ferri in what Bennetts describes as 'a multinational team.' The best results were Keke Rosberg's win at Enna-Pergusa, Sicily, and second place at Donington Park, UK. The same driver also managed to win on the other side of the Atlantic at Westwood in Canada.

American Hugh Bancroft raced Formula Two with Opert that year. He was young and enjoyed partying at least as much as racing. It took a dressing down by Ferri for him to realise that motor racing is a team sport; the mechanics · work hard to prepare a good car, and they don't appreciate a driver turning up still suffering from the effects of the night before, even if he is paying for his drive.

"Bernie was so mad at me for drinking too much the night before a race. He let me have it. We actually shared a room in London. Bernie was fantastic, he was one of the reasons I straightened myself out, and he taught me that it was a team sport."

Ferri was normally a quiet character but he did have a temper, perhaps a legacy of the Italian in his family background. From time to time he would erupt like Vesuvius. One such eruption was caused by the nose cone of a race car. Nose cones on the race cars were made of fibreglass and one particular cone was regularly getting damaged. Each time it came back worse for wear Opert would ask Ferri to fix it, and each time this happened Ferri got madder and madder. Finally the nose cone appeared in pieces one time too many; Opert looked at Ferri and said, "We can fix that," at which point Ferri ran to the nose cone and jumped on it, Opert surveyed the mess of fibreglass and said, "Hmm, I guess we can't fix that."

Hugh Bancroft was a paying driver who had raced Super Vee with Opert in the USA in 1974. He stopped racing in 1975 then returned in '76. For 1977 he told Opert he wanted to race in Formula Two:

"Fred had said to me, 'You know you're going to have a tough time of it.' And he was right, but my time in F2 was the best time of my life."

---

2   Dick Bennetts left NZ in 1972 for a two-year working holiday. After working for Fred Opert over a three-year period he joined Ron Dennis at Project Four Racing. Later he started West Surrey Racing, which he still owns and operates. The company has won five F3 championships and three British Touring Car championships.
    Bennetts remembers that BMW used the NZ series to test their engines. He was told to change engines for different meetings and given the number of the engine that he was to install.

One of Bancroft's memories is their stay at Lord Hesketh's residence, using the 'stables' to prepare their cars.

"It was in the spring of 1977 and the Hesketh Formula One team was out of the country. They had left one of their engineers behind, so he became our host, so to speak. It seems to me it was around the time that we had races at either Brands Hatch, and/or Silverstone. We did not stay there very long, maybe two weeks. If I'm not mistaken we used this as an opportunity to also get the cars prepared to ship to the Continent, as the team would be working out of the transporter for several months. Fred knew just about everybody in racing and he would trade favours with one team or the other."

Bancroft recalls some of the sponsorship that Opert deployed on his cars in both Formula Atlantic and Formula Two.

"Fred had Valvoline on the nose of my car, both for Formula Atlantic and F2. He also had a Girling Brake ad put on a couple of cars that said 'GIRLING, Keeps you up in Front.' Girling was giving us a synthetic brake fluid to try out. Well, over a very short period of time the fluid got past the O-ring seals and we'd lose brake pressure ... end of ad/experiment.

"Fred did a lot of 'private deals' with drivers and their sponsors, by supplying them a car for a given race at God knows what price. We all had different deals. At the end of the day Fred took very good care of us, providing us with well-maintained cars and competent mechanics. His engine of choice was Brian Hart. It was very competitive, but the torquey little 1.5-litre turbo Renaults were tough to keep up with, even for the better drivers."

Bancroft and Gregg Young also raced Opert entries in Formula Libre Shellsport International Championship races. They both raced Chevron B40s with Hart 420R engines. Bancroft considered the two Shellsport races he contested, one at Brands Hatch and one at Thruxton, to be "fillers in:"

"We raced against F1 cars, but it was another point for me to get experience. Brands Hatch was the best track in the UK. I didn't like Silverstone, but I liked Brands."

Bancroft often shared a room with Opert and found his dressing routine hilarious:

"Upon reviewing Fred's obituary, I saw there was a reference to Fred taking every day as a challenge. Hell, Fred started and ended his day with a challenge! Fred always wore square-toed 'cowboy' boots. These boots were the first thing he put on in the morning (after his socks and skivvies). Then he put his pants on. The boots were the last thing that came off at night!

"I'm not sure of the logic here, considering what happened to his feet later on in life, but during my time he might have had a fear of hotel fires! Who knows. There was never a dull moment with Fred."

Bancroft often flew with Opert and, like others, to his amazement he found himself taking American Goodyear tyres on his trans-Atlantic trips as checked baggage.

Back on the road, at Enna-Pergusa in Sicily Keke Rosberg won with a Chevron B40 Hart-engined car. This was cause for great celebration as the little international team had beaten the factory team. On this occasion Rosberg wasn't at all keen at first to race on what was effectively a bowl with a couple of chicanes, and where he was initially getting blown away. However, when Opert arrived he got Rosberg back in the car, the mechanics did their tweaks, and the result was an important victory.

The mechanics had to drive race car trucks and trailers across Europe, which brought all manner of challenges. Dick Bennetts learned the hard way about crossing the border into Italy. The first time he tried, he couldn't understand why he was kept waiting for hours while others seemed to have their papers stamped and were waved through in a matter of minutes. An English truck driver eventually explained what was going on and Bennetts had no trouble after that.

"We always had to have caps and tee shirts for the officials at the Italian border and a carton of cigarettes under the carnets when we handed them over."

Bennetts also recalled their incident-filled trip to Portugal in October 1977.

"We had a dual cab blue and white Chevy with Valvoline advertising that towed three Formula Two cars. But all the weight was over the rear axle, and we broke an axle on the way to Portugal."

In the Portuguese race at Estoril, Rosberg picked up three points for fourth place. There was a time when Portuguese currency was pretty much worthless outside of that country, so rather than change the currency Opert disposed of the team's prize money in a deal for airline tickets which he could, of course, use anywhere.

1977 was also the year that Opert had Eje Elgh drive for him. The men had met two years earlier when Opert and sought out Elgh in the paddock at Zolder, Belgium, and chatted with him. Elgh was still finding his way in the sport and was somewhat overawed that Opert should approach him.

With the help of his countryman, Ronnie Peterson, Elgh became the Chevron Formula Three works driver for 1977. He went into the last round of the British championship with a chance of winning the title along with Derek Daly and Stephen South, but Elgh and South tangled at the first corner allowing Daly to take the race and the title. Elgh and Opert became close friends; it was Elgh who was always on hand to help Opert during his European visits in the years before his death, when he suffered declining health and limited mobility.

In addition to Keke Rosberg, who did 11 races, in '77, Opert ran cars in European Formula Two races for a mixture of other drivers, paying and professional; Hugh 'Wink' Bancroft, Jacques Laffite, Hans Royer, and Gregg Young were entered in multiple races, while Tiff Needell, Alan Jones, Alex Ribeiro, Maurizio Flammini, and Arturo Merzario each did a single race. Alan Jones had completely forgotten about his race for Opert at the Nürburgring, but he had endured a troubled time and finished 18th, so he was probably happy to forget it. Opert rated Jones highly:

"Alan Jones was great: workmanlike, fantastic in my Atlantic car and my Formula Two car. I think a second rank driver, though, even though he was world champion. I don't know, maybe I should take that back. Somehow [Alain] Prost and [Ayrton] Senna seem so fantastic now, and Niki Lauda, that I wouldn't put Alan with Prost, Senna, Niki Lauda or Jackie Stewart, but he'd certainly be there with James Hunt and Keke Rosberg in the second rank, and he was world champion."

Bancroft loved his time in F2 even though, as Opert had predicted, it was tough.

"The Nürburgring was the most amazing track; it took me a month to learn it in a VW Golf. The thing about Fred, he was like a coach. He took you under his wing and he cared about you and looked after things. He had contacts everywhere, I was amazed. He seemed disorganised but he had everything sorted out. He seemed to sleep maybe three hours a night and he always had this great Chinese-looking grin. Being around Fred, there was never a dull moment."

1978 was another year of cross-Atlantic madness for Fred Opert Racing when Rosberg won again at Westwood in Canada, came second at the Nürburgring in Germany, won at Donington Park in England, then went back to Canada where he won at Quebec City and Hamilton, Ontario, and came third in Montreal.

But before that, at the start of 1978, Opert was back in New Zealand to successfully defend the Peter Stuyvesant Series that Rosberg had won the year before.

1978 was the year that Derek Bennett, Chevron's founder and designer, was killed in a hang gliding accident just before the start of the season in March. The start of Opert's Formula Two season was already in disarray, as his new Chevrons were not ready, and only a herculean effort by his own mechanics got cars to Thruxton for the first round; meanwhile the main opposition, in the form of Bruno Giacomelli in a March, had been testing for several months. Opert was convinced that the B42 was not as good as the previous year despite Rosberg achieving good results.

"There's no reason it shouldn't have been a better car, it's just the car didn't get developed properly. We found out at the end of the year we had a worse car than we'd had the year before. It was just that we got better, Keke got better, our team got better, Brian Hart engines got better. I think BMW stagnated and Brian Hart engines got better, so in '78 Derek [Daly] and Keke [Rosberg] were more competitive with the Brian Hart engines."

There was another hectic schedule for Fred Opert Racing in the European Formula Two Championship. This time it was Eje Elgh who did the most races, starting eight times – one more than both Rosberg and Dutchman 'Boy' Hayje. Michael Bleekemolen – another Dutchman – competed in two races, while Arturo Merzario and the future multiple world champion Alain Prost did one race each. This was Prost's first F2 drive and Opert was impressed but didn't have the money to continue the relationship.

Boy Hayje also raced under the Opert umbrella in one round of the Aurora AFX British F1 Championship at Zandvoort in the Netherlands. He finished an impressive third in the Chevron B42-Hart, behind the two Surtees entries of Bob Evans and Divina Galica and ahead of a number of other F1 cars. Despite his Zandvoort result Opert was disappointed with the Dutchman, who he described as very quick, with good car control, but "a complete non-thinker."

Opert entered the Mexican driver Marco Tolama for the 1979 Formula Three race at Monaco. Tolama was racing in the Formula Atlantic series in North America that year, and skipped the Formula Atlantic race at Westwood to enter the Monaco race. He explains how this came about.

"I was anxious that I had lost a lot of time since '71 in England when I was driving Formula Ford. The same thing that happens to a lot of drivers when they run out of money. So I was losing time and I was a little bit anxious to do the most racing that I could. So instead of going to Westwood, Fred convinced Barry Green to rent me his car for the Monaco F3 race. So Fred entered me for the F3 race, but for sure I didn't know what I was getting into, and even though it wasn't that bad, the fact is that I had some seven or eight years that I hadn't run in Europe, and you know how competitive it is, and I had forgotten how the drivers work; and when you have Nigel Mansell, Alain Prost, Stefan Johansson, [Andrea] de Cesaris and so on ... well it wasn't going to be easy.

"It was the year that the Ralt was the chassis to have, and I was running a Barry Green Chevron, so it didn't have the same capabilities; but we were doing okay, except that, during qualifying, twice, Kenny Acheson, an Irishman I think, destroyed my best two qualifying laps, so I couldn't qualify for the race."

There were 55 entries for the 20 positions on the grid, so it is little surprise that Tolama failed to qualify. He was in good company with Thierry Boutsen, Mike Thackwell and Eddie Jordan also failing to make the grid.

Tolama was philosophical about missing the chance to race.

"... you know, it was a good experience. I could run the Monaco track – many, many laps – it was a fantastic experience. Then we came back to keep doing the Formula Atlantic series. Our next Formula Atlantic race was in Quebec, and for sure the experience I had in Monaco helped me a lot, and it was a good race there."

By the end of '78, Opert uncharacteristically described himself as "floundering around." Derek Bennett, the founder and driving force of Chevron, had died, leaving the future of the company in doubt. Rosberg had moved on to Formula One and Can-Am, and Duncan Pitcairn, who was the last junior worker that Opert hired, said that after Derek Bennett's death in '78 "the Opert group drifted apart," and his North American racing operations all but ceased.

Opert was asking himself 'where next?' when the challenge of Formula One Team Management presented itself. He took it. That proved to be a serious mistake.

Fun on Far-flung Shores

Through the mid-to-late '60s Opert had established himself as the biggest importer of formula cars, and as the biggest entrant of those cars at race meetings throughout North America. Promoters in other countries who wanted to attract a field of good racers to their events sought out Opert and invited him, with incentives, to bring his cars and drivers.

In '71 and '72 Opert ventured to Colombia, Venezuela, Mexico, Japan, New Zealand and Australia.

Nick Craw and Bobby Brown both raced in Bogotá early in 1972, when Opert also ran Bert Hawthorne, Brian Robertson, Freddy van Beuren, Rudolfo Junco and Raúl Pérez Gama. Through Opert, new customer John Powell had bought the ex-Redman Chevron B18 at the end of 1971. He lent this car to Brian Robertson to race at the two Bogotá meetings, a week apart, in late February and early March. Powell travelled with the team, and the cars were flown from Miami to Bogotá. Powell remembers it well.

"So we went to Colombia, to Bogotá, this is 1972. What an amazing place, it was just unbelievable. Freddie arranged it all. He had a deal with Marlboro. But first of all, I had to trailer the car down to Miami, then it was put on a plane. We got on the plane and we flew down to Bogotá. We unloaded the cars and put them all together and went to the race track where Brian ran my car. I think he finished a respectable second or third [fifth and second for the two meetings, respectively]. And that was that adventure, and then we all went to the whorehouses.

"It was a typical Freddie deal. It was sponsorship, and you raced with the Hotel Tequendama on the side of the car and in return we got free hotel rooms. I said to Brian, 'Freddie said that you would pay for everything,' and Brian said, 'John, everything I get for free, you get for free.'

"When we were checking out I was watching from a distance as Brian's paying for it all, and he's having a fit and raising his voice, and he never raises his voice. He's getting really angry with the desk clerk because he's trying to check out. There are tourist police with AK47s loitering around. They saunter over and say in Spanish to the desk clerk, 'What's the problem?' He says, 'This guy doesn't want to pay the bill.' And Brian's saying, 'Hey, this is a complimentary room and we put the hotel name on the side of the car.' Anyway, Brian ends up paying. When we're heading back to the airport I said, 'Brian what the hell's going on?' He says, 'They just charged me 1200 US dollars for elevator service!'

"We took a translator – a Phillip Morris lady, because it was a Phillip Morris deal. I'm sitting in the bus talking to her. I said, 'Tell me a little bit about the Hotel Tequendama.' She says, 'Oh, the Hotel Tequendama is owned the Colombian Air Force Officers Retirement Fund. You don't screw around with those people.'"

At the meeting in the last weekend in February Hawthorne won one race and Brown the other, with Hawthorne winning the meeting by dint of his first and second places to Brown's first and third. Van Beuren finished fourth, and Pérez Gama ninth. Hawthorne discovered that his victory had earned him an unexpected bonus: the right to free 'services' at any of the city's brothels.

Bobby Brown won the next weekend, winning both heats, again in a Chevron B20B, with Robertson second, van Beuren sixth and Junco eighth. Hawthorne crashed in the last race.

Opert must have forgotten about the trouble Brian Robertson had at the hotel when he described the trip years later to author David Gordon.

"We had to get the cars as far as the Miami area and we were given so many hotel rooms a car, plus so many meals and transportation for the people and the cars. So all the expenses were pretty much paid. It was a nice junket to go to South America. There was cocaine there in those days and a lot of marijuana, but they hadn't taken over the streets or everything like it is now. We had a wonderful time because Bert Hawthorne won the first race and we became sort of heroes.

"After that, everywhere we went for the next seven days there were parties and just great times. Bert Hawthorne could go into any whorehouse in Bogotá for free! I would say it was one of the more fun things I ever did in racing. The nice thing about it was it was two weeks in succession.

"We sent about seven cars to Bogotá because we had Mexican drivers, American drivers, everyone wanted to drive. We sent every Atlantic we had, either used, new, whatever. I think there were maybe 21 or 22 cars, and seven of them were mine.

"The mechanics took the big truck down there, five of them in a truck and two on another trailer to Miami. And our youngest sort of gopher mechanic, who later became a parts manager, his job was to ride on the freighter from the Colombian air freight company to make sure that nothing was stolen, because we had heard terrible things about the crime and theft in Colombia. They got to Florida and they were two days loading the planes, making sure the cars didn't get destroyed on the plane, and they could see that this was a very bad airline."

Bobby Brown had a great time in Bogotá. He didn't become a regular driver with Opert but they became firm friends, sharing a love of wild times, which included taking Brown's motorhome into New York to try their luck with that city's women. Brown had a house in Brazil that Opert visited several times, including once with his friend, baseball champion Manny Ramirez.

"I had a house in Brazil and Fred came down to visit me. He would come down with Manny Ramirez, who was married to a Brazilian. He [Fred] knew everybody. He was a great guy in every respect but never looked after himself. He had a good sense of humour, but he could be a little overpowering at times."

Because of Opert's strong links with Marlboro, in March 1973 Fred Opert Racing also ventured to Venezuela for the Coppa Presidente de la Republica at Autodromo de San Carlo, Caracas. Rich Jacksic was on the team.

"In Venezuela it was a whole different gang. Gordon Smiley was there. Andrea de Adamich was there because I believe he had ties to Marlboro in Europe. I think he was in F1 at the time. Marlboro was sponsoring the races in Colombia and Venezuela. So I guess he had to come over. A very nice guy … great, great guy.

"We had Carl Liebich from Wisconsin there, and Bill O'Connor. They were winter-time races, and down there it was a big deal. In Venezuela we had all the Mexicans. We had, Freddy van Beuren, Raúl Pérez Gama, Mauricio Calderón and Ernesto Soto."

Fred Opert Racing had seven entries in the 16 car field, including Marlboro-sponsored Formula One driver Andrea de Adamich, who won both races to take the overall win ahead of two other Opert drivers, Carl Liebich and Bobby Dennett.

Opert may have promised the organisers a field of international entries; Carl Liebich arrived to find himself entered as German, and Bill O'Connor as Irish. Liebich was on the podium twice, which caused the organisers some consternation as they scurried around to find a copy of the German national anthem, which Liebich wouldn't have recognised anyway.

When he returned home, Liebich received a call from a woman with a thick German accent. She explained that she was from the German consulate and that they had noted that he had gone to Venezuela, but when they checked their records, they had no information about his initial entry into the USA. Liebich tried to explain that he wasn't German and the circumstances of his 'German' entry in the races. Finally, after much toing and froing, the woman advised that he would have to speak with the consul. There was a pause before Opert's laughter echoed down the line.

John Powell was also on the Venezuelan trip, he took the Brabham BT38 that Opert had purchased on his behalf from Ron Dennis. He remembers that when the cars were unloaded from the ship, they were full of coffee beans, which they had to empty out. He thinks the dockworkers simply put the cars into the hold then poured a load of coffee beans into the same hold.

Colombia and Venezuela were exotic trips for the team, a rare opportunity to visit countries that would soon become too dangerous for such adventures.

On the other side of the world, after the demise of the Tasman Series in New Zealand and Australia (which had been enjoyed by Formula One drivers in their European off-season), the two 'Down Under' countries continued to run series that attracted international drivers to their sunny shores. In the first half of the 1970s Formula 5000 was the chosen category. The New Zealand race series started on the first days of each year.

For the 1976 F5000 series in New Zealand, Ron Frost, who was the President of the Motorsport Association of New Zealand, invited Opert to enter a car. Brian Redman was to be the driver.

Frost (who later received an MBE) was the leading figure in putting New Zealand on the world motorsport stage, with his promotion of the famous Tasman Series and subsequent single-seater series. Brian Redman recalls:

"We were supposed to take an F5000 car, but at the last minute the deal fell apart and Fred asked if BMW would lend me a couple of 2-litre motors as he could get a Chevron F2 car. So that's what happened. We had a very good mechanic, New Zealander Dick Bennetts.

"I was mildly surprised when Fred asked if I could find any sponsorship. I had never done that as, since 1968, I had been lucky enough to drive for factory teams where that wasn't needed."

If there was criticism of Opert turning up with a Formula Two car for a F5000 series, it was quietened by Redman's performances in the Chevron B29, which included a fourth at the New Zealand Grand Prix and a second at Manfeild – in the south of the North Island – on a tight track and a wet day that suited the small car. Mechanical problems conspired against other good results, with a rod going through the BMW block during the Lady Wigram Trophy race in Christchurch when well placed, and a broken wheel at Teretonga.

When he was interviewed after his retirement from the race in Christchurch, Redman quipped:

"We had an electrical problem ... a rod knocked the starter motor cable off."

Perhaps it was a combination of the Fred Opert grin and Brian Redman's engaging personality that won everyone over. Whatever it was, Opert and Frost did a deal for the following year that resulted in Keke Rosberg's championship. Did Opert and Frost have a good relationship? Kiwi racer and joint Tiga founder, Howden Ganley, thought that might have been a stretch:

"'Good' is probably relative. If you were 'in' with him [Frost] you got a good deal, but not everyone found him easy to deal with. I certainly didn't – and I have detailed my very unsatisfactory dealings with him in my book[1]. BRM tired of him as well, and I wonder how things went with Bruce [McLaren] too.

---

1 *The Road to Monaco* by Howden Ganley, published by Denley Publications.

"Fred was enough of a 'wheeler-dealer' that he probably figured out how to maximise the travel money Frost was offering."

Redman and Opert enjoyed their time in New Zealand, and Redman tells a story of being at the Teretonga track near Invercargill, which is on the southernmost tip of New Zealand's South Island.

"When we were in Invercargill, a pretty remote spot, I mentioned to Fred that the BMW motor seemed to be revving higher than the rev counter indicated (we used 10,000rpm). Joking, Fred turned to a spectator and asked if there was a Smith's instrument test station anywhere nearby.

"'Yes mate,' came the response. 'Go down main street, turn right at the bottom, and it's on the left!'

"And, yes, the rev counter was reading 500rpm too low."

At the start of 1977 Fred Opert Racing contested the New Zealand Peter Stuyvesant Series for Formula Pacific cars with Keke Rosberg and Mikko Kozarowitzky in Chevron B34s. Opert had planned to take Kozarowitzky – who had Marlboro sponsorship – and English driver Ian Grob, but that deal fell through, so he called Rosberg just days before the first race and asked him to fly over. Rosberg got some money from his sponsor, Warsteiner, then Opert found local New Zealand sponsors to help finance Rosberg's car.

After his long flight Rosberg emerged from the quiet terminal building to find a Ford Model T waiting for him. After initially thinking he had travelled through a time-warp, Rosberg discovered that Opert was behind the prank, having arranged for the local Ford dealer to pick Rosberg up in the Model T.

Rosberg travelled at a less sedate pace on the track, taking three wins and a second in the five-round series to win the championship, ahead of Tom Gloy in a Tui. No doubt the prize money helped defray Opert's costs. Kozarowitzky was fourth.

Rosberg loved his Chevron B34.

"I believe that the '77 car was a real Chevron: easy to set up, easy to understand. The '78 car [B39] was not so forgiving and was much more difficult to set up."

New Zealand champion David Oxton summed up Rosberg's Stuyvesant Championships.

"Rosberg was great for New Zealand, and New Zealand was great for him. He was as flamboyant and charming as any sportsman/superstar – but ruthless and absolutely uncompromising. Talents which, no doubt, helped him to become world champion."

Tom Hooker, who still runs a specialist engine building business in Indianapolis, had worked for Opert in 1976 but returned to New Zealand for the birth of his first child. When Opert sent cars and engines to New Zealand it was Hooker he hired to freshen them up. The engines were stock-block 1600cc engines with twin Weber carburettors instead of the full-race, BMW fuel-injected engines that Opert had used in Redman's car in '76. After preparing the cars, Hooker then joined Dick Bennetts and the team for the Peter Stuyvesant Series. He was a fan of Rosberg, but was not so enamoured with Kozarowitzky.

"That Kozarowitzky, he was a pain in the arse. He had Marlboro sponsorship. He thought he was the world's next F1 champion. He did have the most glorious Finnish wife though. God, she was stunning. He was hopeless. I think it was at Puke [Pukekohe, near Auckland], he even got to the point where he was bitching up a storm that Keke had a better engine than he had. So we said, 'Okay.' We didn't have to, but we pulled both engines while he stood there. We swapped both engines over, and Keke still blew him into the dust. So that shut him up.

"The last race at Wigram, we were staying at the White Heron Motor Inn in Christchurch. He didn't have the balls to say 'Thanks guys,' he just left the track and said nothing and went back to the hotel. So we got back to the hotel, and we'd had a couple of beers by then, and we said, 'Right, we're really going to give him a send-off.' We went to his room, knocked on the door and his wife came and said, 'He's in the shower,' and we said 'Oh, good.' So we went into the shower, grabbed him – he's yelling and screaming – we threw a towel over his midrift and held him above us. We walked through the restaurant with him naked, yelling and screaming. We walked out through the doors to the pool, threw him in the pool and walked away. We never saw or heard from him again. That fixed him. All the people that were dining there, were, 'Wow! What's going on here?'"

Years later, Kozarowitzky's son, Nikolai, became an important part of Opert's life.

At the start of 1978, Opert and Rosberg were back in New Zealand to defend their Peter Stuyvesant Series championship. Tom Hooker had remained in New Zealand, where Opert had left the engines from the previous year, which once again he freshened up ready for the series (Bobby Rahal reported that he took engines for his car with him, so perhaps Hooker only prepared Rosberg's). He and Dick Bennetts were once again the main mechanics for the team.

Five internationals joined 15 Kiwis and three Aussies for the series. The smart booklet that was the souvenir programme for the series (which cost the princely sum of one New Zealand dollar) contained the following comment on Fred Opert's arrival:

"Racing patron Fred Opert arrived on these shores with his unmistakable grin. To those who know Fred the grin means one of two things – if he gives you 'the grin' after he has spoken to you then he has won his bet – and if he gives you 'the grin' before he speaks to you then he knows he is going to win the bet. It's like having the title rights to second place."

It is unlikely that Fred would have welcomed being described as a 'racing patron.' He ran a business and had a rule that he did not invest his own money in racing, although he had broken that rule to ensure that Rosberg could continue his European F2 racing in a competitive car.

This time American Bobby Rahal[2] was Rosberg's teammate, both men driving Chevron B39s. Rosberg won the series for a second time. Bobby Rahal enjoyed himself and came third.

"I went to New Zealand in 1978 with Fred. That was the start of our professional relationship. I had engines that my sponsor let me take to compete in the series. I remember that everyone in New Zealand was very welcoming, there were lots of parties."

Opert commented on Rosberg's treatment of his Chevron B39 at the first round of the series at Baypark Raceway, where Rosberg won the second heat.

"The real funny thing with Keke that we could never figure out; when he won the first race in New Zealand, at Baypark [January '78], Dick Bennetts was head mechanic on the New Zealand teams, and Keke jumped out of the car and got up on the victory dais, and Dick and I went to push the car into the parc fermé, and we couldn't push it, it wouldn't roll. The wheels were so bent they were hitting the brake callipers. There were a lot of kerbs at Baypark and he had bent the wheels so bad that with 200 horsepower, you could turn the wheels, but two men couldn't push the car.

"So we had to get permission to start it and drive it over to the impound area. What took me about eight months to figure out with him is why he bent the inside of the wheels. It's very easy to bend an outside, you hit a kerb or something. What he would do was, if there was, say, a left-hand corner, he would lift the left front wheel high enough, so it would go over the speed bumps all the way. He'd get the car in an attitude, so the car was past the speed bump in the air, but if it dropped a little bit it would graze the inside edge of the wheel.

"We always used three-piece wheels with Keke for a couple of reasons. Now everybody uses three-piece wheels, but we were one of the first teams. Money-wise it was only $100 a wheel to put a side piece on, where it was like $700 to buy a new wheel. But more important, on the street circuits, when you bent a three-piece wheel it bent, whereas if you had a one-piece cast wheel and you hit the kerb a piece fell out of it and the tyre would go flat and you'd have to make a pit stop."

In November of '78, after a six-year break, Formula Two returned to Argentina for the Temporada with just two races, the first in Mendoza, the second in Buenos Aires. Opert ran Keke Rosberg in his Chevron B42 – controversially using

---

2   Bobby Rahal would later go on to a stellar career in IndyCar after two outings for Wolf in Formula One. He won the Indianapolis 500 in 1986 plus three IndyCar CART championships and 24 races. He is now principal at Rahal Letterman Lanigan Racing.

American Goodyear tyres. All the other teams were using Goodyears supplied by International Race Tire Service, owned by Bernie Ecclestone. They were limited to two sets per car due to supply problems. But Opert had a long-standing relationship with Goodyear in the USA and saw no reason why he should pay Ecclestone for his tyres. On the track the March cars dominated and the Opert cars were not competitive.

Tom Hooker reported that Opert sent two cars to New Zealand for the 1979 Formula Pacific Series, which he thinks were the pink cars sponsored by Durex Excita condoms. He believes that Opert couldn't find drivers and, in the end, the cars weren't used. So that was the end of Opert's New Zealand adventures.

The Asian gambling hub of Macau holds an annual street race on a very demanding circuit. These races attract top drivers from across the globe. One of the more unusual rent-a-drive deals for Opert was in 1979 at Macau. British racing driver Rupert Keegan was starring in Formula Three, and his father (Mike Keegan, owner of TransMeridian Airlines) did a deal with Opert for a car for Rupert to race in Macau. The team that ran Keegan in F3 in the UK effectively ran the car for him but Tom Hooker built an engine for the car:

"Fred did a deal with Rupert Keegan to go to Macau. You could run a big valve, 1600cc, fuel-injected engine at Macau. Of course, Fred didn't have any 1600 injected engines, so I just built a big valve carburettor engine and took that over to England and went up to Chevron's – Fred was running F2 in those days as well – and Dick Bennetts was working for him then, doing the F2."

Hooker went to Macau with the car as Fred's representative:

"Fred owned the car. The team that used to run Rupert in F3 in those times, they ran the car for him. I just had to go as Fred's representative, but I ended up working on the car. Keegan's old man was very gruff. Macau has a huge long front straightaway, and as the car was going down the front straightaway you'd hear the odd miss. When I walked back along the pits Keegan's old man grabbed me and said, 'What the fuck's wrong with that car?' I said, 'Nothing that I know of.' And he said, 'Well, what's that miss?' I don't know why I thought of it, but the F2 cars had a switch on the steering wheel that overrode the rev limiter, I just leaned in and switched that off and the thing was perfect for the rest of the week. I was pretty pleased about that!"

In what was probably another of Opert's travel deals, Hooker – who had flown to Macau with Lufthansa – had to go back to the UK in one of Mike Keegan's freighters, with the car and a full load of general freight. Keegan's TransMeridian Airlines used CL44 cargo planes: four-engine prop planes that he used for freight between Hong Kong and Europe. The trip took several days via Hong Kong, Kuala Lumpur, Delhi, Africa, Turkey, Amsterdam, and then Stansted in England. There was only one pilot (no relief crew) and the plane could only take off at night from hot countries because temperature was critical at take-off. It was a long but interesting trip back for Hooker.

The Macau deal for Keegan might have been the last of its type that Opert did, as '79 was the year that he briefly managed the ATS F1 team before returning to the USA and his road car import/export business.

Friendships and a Championship

Fred Opert had an ability to spot and engage talented drivers early in their careers. Many champions and future champions drove for Fred Opert Racing, including: Alan Jones, Jacques Laffite, Jean-Pierre Jarier, Alain Prost, Bobby Rahal, Didier Pironi, Peter Gethin, Brian Redman, Héctor Rebaque, Bertil Roos, Rolf Stommelen, Patrick Tambay, Rupert Keegan, Derek Daly, Danny Sullivan, Reine Wisell, Tim Schenken, and Bert Hawthorne.

Of all the men who drove for Opert, two became lifelong friends: Keke Rosberg and Eje Elgh.

Keke Rosberg is the name that first comes to mind when enthusiasts talk of Fred Opert. Theirs was a special affinity – a friendship beyond the normal driver/team owner relationship.

It seems most likely that Ian Williams of Tui racing cars was the matchmaker between Opert and Rosberg (Duncan Pitcairn, who worked for Opert, thought that a mechanic of Bertil Roos had introduced them, but given that Opert was running Roos in a Tui Formula Super Vee it could be that Pitcairn was referring to Williams). In 1974 Williams had suggested that Opert take an interest in the Super Vee performances of Rosberg. In turn Williams also encouraged Rosberg to introduce himself to Opert by writing to him. Opert referred to this in his interview with author David Gordon.

"Keke wrote me a letter from Finland, saying that he was a Super Vee driver ... he wrote me a couple of times, and then I ran into him at the [London Olympia] Racing Car Show. I'd wanted to meet him. I still hadn't seen him drive. Then that spring I'd seen him drive in Super Vee a couple of times when we were at Hockenheim or Nürburgring. He didn't have the best car, he had a Kaimann, but he was quite a good driver. At the end of '75, Ian Williams convinced me to try him at the Glen; there was a preliminary to the Grand Prix of the United States at Watkins Glen and it was very important for Ian, so I brought over a brand new Super Vee. I remember it was red and on the side it says, 'K K Rosberg!' It was like Kevin Karl and when he arrived he got a laugh out of that.

"We had a great time that weekend, I remember; a fantastic time. There were a lot of pretty girls around and it was a very good weekend. But Keke only finished fifth in the Super Vee race – the car didn't suit him, the track, or maybe we didn't have the best engine – I don't know what it was, but he finished fifth … I was still quite impressed with him."

For 1976 Rosberg drove Jörg Obermoser's Formula Two TOJ, but he struggled to qualify the uncompetitive car. For Estoril, with some financial help from his sponsor Warsteiner, he had a one-off drive with Fred Opert Racing in José Dolhem's Chevron B35. The difference was immediate, as the Finn qualified third fastest with his Hart-engined Chevron ahead of the Chevron BMW-powered works car driven by Hans Binder. René Arnoux cleared out in the lead while Rosberg and Alex Ribeiro fought over second place. Sadly, a water pipe let go on the Chevron and Rosberg failed to finish. He was bitterly disappointed, but his performance had attracted attention.

Fred Opert planned to start 1977 in New Zealand competing with two Chevron B34s. Marlboro sponsored Mikko Kozarowitzky, who had won the European Formula Super Vee championship in 1975, beating none other than Keke Rosberg. Kozarowitzky had suffered a disastrous year in F2, and Marlboro approached Opert to run him in New Zealand. The New Zealand series was sponsored by Peter Stuyvesant, so the car could not appear in Marlboro colours but Kozarowitzky could wear his Marlboro race suit and other apparel.

Rosberg knew of Opert's plans but was unable to come up with enough sponsorship from Warsteiner to pay for the trip. Rosberg recalls:

"I never discussed financial issues with him [Fred] but when, I think it was end of '76, when I wanted to go with him to New Zealand, I couldn't because he couldn't afford it. We had to agree that it wasn't going to work, and then it was very lucky for me that the guy who had agreed to come couldn't find the money, so Fred called me, like Christmas Eve, and said, 'can you be down here in two days?' So again, for sure, that cost him money, but we managed to get quite a lot of sponsors in New Zealand along the way during the series, and we won the series and that was a very lucky break for me. It was the best time in motor racing for Fred and for me. We loved it."

Opert provided additional details when he was interviewed about the arrangements.

"On Christmas Eve 1976, I called Keke Rosberg in Heidelberg and asked if there was any way he could find a sponsor so that he could drive the second car in the New Zealand series. The only thing that he could come up with was US$5000 from Warsteiner Beer, who had sponsored him in the one race he had driven for me in Portugal earlier that year. I took a chance that we could pick up other sponsors when we arrived in New Zealand, as I was really keen on having Keke on my team."

The Peter Stuyvesant Series in New Zealand offered five race meetings over five consecutive weekends, starting at Baypark Raceway on January 3rd 1977, in sunny Mount Maunganui on the east coast of the North Island.

Rosberg won three rounds of the series, including the New Zealand Grand Prix at Pukekohe close to Auckland, and he clinched the championship at the other end of the country at Teretonga, with one race still to be run. He was leading that final race until he had to pit with a puncture, but he still finished second to Tom Gloy.

Opert commented, "... the mechanics loved him, everything was good, he was good with sponsors."

Opert and Rosberg might have seemed a natural partnership after their 1977 success in New Zealand, and they did discuss doing Formula Two together, but a lack of money seemed to scuttle the idea. When Opert did eventually call Rosberg in the middle of the night to tell him that he did want to run him in F2, Rosberg had already signed for his friend Jörg Obermoser to race his TOJ. He was in Heidelberg to test the TOJ at Hockenheim.

Opert had broken his golden rule, he was willing to spend his own money to run Rosberg, and Rosberg had to break a contract with his friend if he wanted to drive a competitive car in F2.

"It was a terrible decision for me. But really it was a decision I had to take; am I going to become an international racing driver, or am I going to go down the drain? The decision was correct but it was a tough one. I sacrificed a friend on the way to becoming an international racing driver. The decision was correct, but you can never say it's worth it."

To manage his budgets in such a way that he could afford to run Rosberg in F2, Opert needed him to also race in the Atlantic series in Canada. For the rest of 1977 Rosberg raced another 21 events – five Formula Atlantic, 15 Formula Two, and Macau. He says; "... it was the most hectic time ever."

Although he didn't win either the Atlantic or F2 series Rosberg featured strongly, winning at Westwood in Canada and giving Fred Opert Racing its first European F2 victory at Enna-Pergusa in Sicily. It was a very special win for Opert.

"It was probably, at that point, the biggest day of my life, winning Enna. For an American team to come over and win – no American team had ever won a Formula Two race in the history of Formula Two. It wasn't really American, except for me, and the bank account was American, but I considered it an American team. To go over and win was very exciting."

Dick Bennetts recalls the Enna event:

"We got there later than most of the other teams. It's just a bowl with a couple of Chicanes. Fred hadn't arrived when Keke took the car out. He pulled back in, got out of the car and said, 'We're wasting our time. We are just getting blown away.' I protested, telling him that we had only just arrived and hadn't started car set-up. But he was adamant. So I said, 'Okay, we're happy to enjoy the sunshine.' It was actually extremely hot.

101

"When Fred arrived in the afternoon he wanted to know why we weren't running. I suggested he go and have a chat to his driver. He got Keke back into the car, we did wing adjustments and chassis tuning, and Keke won the race!

"We prepared our cars at the Chevron factory in Bolton, but there was a bit of rivalry between us and the factory team. Paul Owens was always going on about having the best car and driver. After Enna I made some comment about how good a little private team with a ragtag bunch of internationals was. That didn't go down too well."

Bennetts enjoyed working for Rosberg but wished he had been easier on the equipment.

"We had Speedline rims, and on one occasion we went through 12 in one weekend. I tried to warn Keke but he kept using the kerbs and ended up breaking the suspension."

In 1978 Rosberg must have been the race driver who covered the most miles in the sky as he contested the European Formula Two championship as well as the Formula Atlantic Labatts Championship Series in Canada for Fred Opert Racing, plus he ran in Formula One for Theodore, ATS and Wolf. Keke recalls:

"I was the most travelled driver in the world by a country mile. In '78 I think I ran 41 races on five different continents, or something like that. I was so busy travelling I wasn't short of cash because I didn't need any. I was either in an airport or a hotel. I have no recollection how the financial side worked. Did I make money from Fred, or did I not? I have no idea."

An example of Rosberg's hectic schedule in 1978 was during the first weeks of July when, on the first weekend, he practiced in France at Circuit Paul Ricard in the F1 ATS, then flew to the USA for a mid-week meeting at Lime Rock, where he wrote off a B45 in practice before taking over Eje Elgh's car for the race to finish sixth. He then flew back to Europe for an F2 race at Nogaro, France, where he had a DNF while lying eighth.

As well as New Zealand, F2 in Europe, and Formula Atlantic in Canada, 1978 was the year when the pair competed in the Argentine Temporada (Mendoza and Buenos Aires), and Macau.

"His [Fred's] briefcase held one or two bunches of airplane tickets held together with a rubber band. I remember we were in Germany one time at a race and the next week I had to be at Elkhart Lake [Wisconsin]. He took this bunch of tickets out and said, 'Here, I have a Frankfurt to Atlanta ticket that hasn't been used.' And I said, 'Fred I don't want to go to Atlanta,' and he said, 'Use that and then we use the other end from this other ticket ...' And in those days nothing was checked like it is today.

"He bought all his tickets in a travel agency run by two Pakistani guys in London, they had the best deals in the world on airline tickets and Fred was better than any travel agent to organise things."

"In those days DHL didn't deliver all the equipment to the paddock like they do now for F1. Fred was his own boss ... solo entrepreneur. At JFK you just labelled your luggage at the roadside at the terminal. Fred would turn up at the terminal with Goodyear tyres, two nose cones, one gearbox. He'd pay the luggage boy $100 and say, 'Put labels on those,' and Fred was on his way. But you can imagine the faces at customs in Europe when all this stuff arrived at this end with absolutely no papers ..."

On the matter of Opert spending his own money to run him in F2, Rosberg said:

"I never asked him where the money came from. I would assume he put money in, because we didn't have much money. Eje [Elgh] was in the other car, he had good money[1] and there was a Dutch guy in the third car [Boy Hayje]. I think basically he juggled around with all those monies and financed my car. I never discussed financial issues with him.

"There was also a deep feeling of gratefulness because I knew he couldn't afford to run me. It started with the F2 deal in '77, which we both knew was a disaster in the making because he didn't have the money, and then bit, by bit, by bit, we went through the whole season, which was amazing.

"Fred didn't pay me. His job was to bring me a car, and my job was to find sponsors and get patches on my overalls. At the end of that long year it was back to New Zealand, and we won the series again."

Other than some sponsorship from his long-time supporter Valvoline, Fred was using his own money to run Rosberg. Author David Gordon describes the Fred Opert Racing's F2 campaign:

"... the entire operation was a masterpiece of organisation as Opert worked out of hotel rooms and airport lounges. His travel arrangements were especially legendary. He always seemed to carry a wad of leftover airline tickets which he had obtained at virtually no cost. All you needed to be able to use them was an atlas, as Rosberg explains:

"'From Frankfurt to Chicago, there's a non-stop flight. Except, when I went with Fred's ticket it took me 24 hours to get there. Fred would get you at the cheapest rate from A to B, but mostly you had to go via Z and X.'"

Rosberg delivered Chevron's last Formula Two win at Donington on June 25, 1978, in the Hart-engined B42. But the funds were drying up and Rosberg was struggling with the impact of the endless travel (it was reported that he spent 420 hours in aeroplanes that year), so Opert decided to concentrate on the Formula Atlantic Championship, although they did run Formula Two in Argentina and Macau. Rosberg only managed ninth place in Mendoza and eighth in Buenos Aires.

---

1   Eje Elgh had sponsorship from Marlboro arranged by Fred through John Hogan, the Marlboro sponsorship manager.

Opert explained the dilemma that faced the pair when Formula Two and Formula Atlantic race dates clashed:

"Around mid-season we knew there were about four conflicts coming up. There were only so many weekends and it really wasn't possible to run both series, so we had to make a decision.

"In fact, he [Rosberg] would have preferred to run Formula Two than Atlantic 'cause more of the right press could see him in Formula Two and it was obviously a much better stepping stone to Formula One. But we obviously had no chance to win the Formula Two Championship."

A decision had to be made in July as the F2 race at Misano on August 6th clashed with the Formula Atlantic race in Hamilton, Ontario. Opert:

"If he did well in Ontario he could maybe win the Atlantic championship. He didn't like the decision really, he would rather have continued in Formula Two and get some finishes there. He felt like a second and third in Formula Two was better than winning the Atlantic championship."

Rosberg won in Hamilton and took the lead in the Atlantic championship. The final race in the series would be at Île Notre-Dame in Quebec. But it was Opert who now had a conflict; he needed to be at Hockenheim for the last F2 race of the season, where he had three cars entered. When Opert left Canada he was happy that Rosberg had the fastest car, but in the race disaster struck when a spark plug broke. Rosberg finished 21st and the championship was lost. Opert was deeply disappointed, but failing to win that championship did not damage Rosberg's Formula One aspirations. It was another of Opert's contacts who helped in Rosberg's move to F1.

For years Marlboro used motorsport as a major part of its marketing programme. The Australian John Hogan looked after Marlboro's investments in the sport, and was influential in Formula One for more than three decades. He first met Opert in 1971 when he was with the Rondel Formula Two team run by Ron Dennis and Neil Trundle. He held Opert in high regard as a talent spotter.

"Fred was the go-to guy if we were looking to place young drivers. He was always friendly and always 100 per cent reliable. I liked him a lot."

The two men worked together on a number of occasions, including when Rosberg was trying to establish himself in Formula One.

"Getting Keke Rosberg into Formula One, it was so complicated I can't remember all of it now, but he was driving Teddy [Theodore] Yip's car and we put in a bit of money. He was driving it at Hockenheim and he did very well, and I think it was that that put Keke on the map.

"That's Fred, he took people under his wing, not just for pure business purposes – he had to like you."

Rosberg's move to Formula One in 1979 meant that he ceased racing for Opert (as well as Formula One he also raced Can-Am sports cars). Nevertheless, the pair remained close, with Rosberg having an involvement in Opert's move into F1 team management with ATS.

"I suppose I was part of Fred's move to the ATS team. I had raced a lot in Germany. It was a great opportunity for Fred, and was seen as such, but of course the owner of ATS was the most difficult man on earth [Hans Günter Schmid]. That was well known, but I thought, and Fred thought, that he could handle it with his personality. But didn't work very well, and they fell apart big time, which left Fred in limbo because he had stopped his own racing in order to do this.

"I think after ATS he wasn't racing again. He went back to deal in cars and he spent a lot of time in Florida with his dad, who was still alive. He was very caring about his old dad and we had a close contact somehow, probably on the phone, because I know all that."

In fact, Opert did continue to run cars in the North American Formula Atlantic series throughout 1979, but disappeared from the entry lists after the first race of 1980.

So what was Opert's view of Rosberg the driver? In an interview with David Gordon in '89 he provided this summary:

"Keke had almost too much confidence in himself. Very cocky, had all the confidence. Incredible car control, and very brave. Could learn a circuit instantly.

"I would think if you took a car like a new Japanese Formula One car that no-one had ever seen before, let's say it had been tested by Japanese drivers so it at least would turn left and right, and you went to a strange circuit in Paraguay, so no-one had seen the circuit and nobody had ever driven the car, and you could pick any ten drivers you wanted – Ron Dennis can pick any ten drivers he wants and I'll take Keke. If each guy gets ten laps in the car, Keke will be faster. What I'm saying is, the guy could really go fast and he could do it in anything, wherever."

A new chapter in their relationship opened when Rosberg's son Nico was born, and when Opert became an uncle to his brother Larry's son, Derek.

"Basically, when my son [Nico] was born then the relationship was refreshed big time."

Derek Opert and Nico Rosberg became friends, and Fred followed Nico's Formula One career with a passion – a passion that might have bought about his untimely death.

In 2016 Fred travelled to Budapest then Germany to see Nico race in what became his championship year, but he was very ill and should not have travelled.

Rosberg saw Opert in Germany at his friend Andreas Mann's house.

"Eje Elgh was the one who looked after Fred towards the end. When he really needed care at the Grands Prix, Eje looked after him. He was an ex-driver of Fred's.

105

"Fred was hospitalised in Budapest, then he left the hospital against all advice to go to Hockenheim, and I stopped him in his tracks at his friend's [Andreas Mann] place. I said, 'Fred you are not going to a race, you are not in that condition. You are an embarrassment to yourself and to everybody else.' He actually accepted that and admitted that I was right. I said to him, 'You go home now, go to the doctor, get yourself sorted out and go to the USA Grand Prix in Austin when you are back on your own feet and you are fit again.' And he said, 'Yes you are right, that's what I am going to do.' I'm happy because I stopped him. Somebody had to do it. I think I did it [while] embracing him. And luckily, he called me [from the USA], and we had this last call and there were no hard feelings. He understood. He knew I was right."

So Rosberg's last time with his friend was stressful, but true friends sometimes have to be brutally honest with each other, as was the case with Rosberg and Opert in Germany. At least the friends spoke again when Opert called a few days before he died.

The other driver that Opert was close to was Eje Elgh. He was a Swedish racing driver who raced in a number of categories of formula cars and sports cars, in many countries, from 1974 to 1992. Elgh had become a close friend of Opert, and in Opert's last years, when he was suffering serious health issues that limited his mobility, Elgh looked after him when Opert attended Grands Prix.

Like many young boys who dream of becoming a racing driver, Elgh raced go-karts when he was young. Fellow Swede, Ronnie Peterson, was his hero when he was growing up. Elgh worked and borrowed money to get his first race car in 1974, a Formula Super Vee, which he bought from another countryman – future Lotus Formula One driver Gunnar Nilsson[2], who delivered it to him.

Elgh raced the car in Europe. He also discovered that the Super Vee category was running in the United States. He had heard Opert's name and found out about his racing school in Pocono. Bertil Roos, another Swedish driver, worked there and sometimes drove Super Vees for Opert. So even though Elgh hadn't met Opert, he knew of him.

Around this time Elgh became friends with Keke Rosberg, a friendship that grew to be very strong and still survives. Rosberg talked a lot to Elgh about Opert.

In Elgh's second year he bought a Lola and started to get some good results, and he met Opert for the first time.

"Fred was someone who became very close to me from the first day. I met Fred at Zolder in Belgium in 1975. He came to talk to me, and he showed interest in me by just coming and talking. I didn't really take anything else out of it, but Fred was a

---

2   Nilsson died of cancer in 1978. He raced in 32 Grands Prix, winning the Belgium GP for Lotus in
    1977.

big name, and for me it was a big thing that he came and talked to me. After that I kept my ears and eyes open and was aware of what Fred was doing."

In 1976 Elgh was signed to drive for Viking, a Swedish Formula Three team. He sold his own race car, but he only managed a couple of races before Viking went bankrupt. He rented his old car back from its new German owner and managed a few races but with little success.

The next year, Swedish driver Ronnie Peterson and his manager took Elgh under their wings. They took him to the Chevron factory. Elgh says that Peterson disappeared into an office, so he wandered off to look around the factory, recalling "I didn't have a clue what was going on." When Peterson reappeared, and they were on their way back, he asked Elgh, "So, how do you feel about being a works driver in Formula Three?" That's how Elgh came to drive for Chevron in 1977.

At Oulton Park, Elgh led a Formula Three race in the pouring rain, and won his first race in the British F3 championship ahead of Derek Warwick. From then on, he was racing for the championship.

Elgh's car was normally a pale blue, but at Monaco, in May of that year, it was primarily red when it rolled out of the trailer, as a result of Marlboro sponsorship that Peterson had organised. "Apparently I was now a Marlboro driver. So I was part of the Marlboro World Championship Team." This was a big deal for Elgh, akin to being supported by Red Bull in modern times.

It wasn't long before Elgh found himself with a Formula Two drive.

"At the end of the season I was suddenly called in to the [Phillip Morris] office in England. It was run by an Australian guy, John Hogan, the top man in the Marlboro racing world. When I came in, there was John Hogan and Fred Opert sitting at the table and they told me that I would race in Formula Two at Estoril at the end of the season, and that's really where my story with Fred starts. He had got some money out of Marlboro, I suppose, and he put me in the third car. There was Keke and perhaps someone else [Hugh Bancroft]."

In those days Formula One drivers also ran in F2, so it was a very competitive category. Elgh did race at Estoril, an attractive beach resort just 22 kilometres east of Lisbon in an area known as the Portuguese Riviera. He started 12th and finished eighth. He was disappointed with that result, but Opert and Hogan were happy with his performance. It was his first F2 race and the drivers who finished ahead of him included Pironi, Arnoux, Rosberg, Cheever, Daly and Patrese. American Hugh 'Wink' Bancroft was the third Opert entry for that race, but failed to qualify.

"At Estoril, it was the first time that I spent some time with Fred and he had his dad there, and perhaps [his brother] Larry and his [Fred's] wife was there as well. We were there for a week. It was nice weather and we stayed close to the circuit. I felt like I was treated like one of the Opert family."

During the winter a deal was worked out for Elgh to take part in the European F2 championship with Fred Opert Racing alongside Rosberg and Dutch driver Boy Hayje.

Despite Opert's relationship with Chevron the team's new B42 cars were delivered very late (this was shortly after Chevron owner, Derek Bennett, had been killed in a hang gliding accident). The drivers did a few shakedown laps at Silverstone before heading to Thruxton for the first race. Elgh thinks that neither he or Rosberg qualified – there were around 50 cars entered for 30 spots on the grid – but other reports show Rosberg as being in the race but not finishing due to an electrical fault, and Hayje finishing 11th in a Chevron B42-Hart.

"We never got the cars running properly and somehow, we didn't qualify. It was like a big eye opener, but it was going to get even worse because the next race was the following weekend, or two weeks later at Hockenheim, and I didn't qualify there either. I just couldn't get around some of the characteristics of the car. I remember blaming one thing after another. Keke qualified and was running in the front so there was nothing wrong with the car."

In the race at Hockenheim Rosberg qualified on the front row and finished eighth after suffering a slowly deflating tyre. Hayje finished 16th.

Things did get better for Elgh when he finished ninth at the Nürburgring. Rosberg finished second. Then on the streets of Pau in the south of France, Elgh scored his first F2 podium – a second place behind Marc Surer. Another champion of the future was also entered in one of Opert's cars for that race, Alain Prost, but he failed to finish and Opert's funds didn't stretch to adding Prost to his team.

Adversity strengthened the relationship between Elgh and Opert later in the year at Donington. Elgh remembers:

"I was qualifying and I crashed very, very heavily, and I destroyed the car completely. I thought, this is probably the end of my F2, but Fred just got a me a new car. I was very well looked after by Fred. I'm talking about 1978, and this was the foundation of my relationship to Fred."

Any angst that Opert felt about the destroyed car was probably offset by Rosberg's win at Donington. Elgh reflected on his experience:

"When I look back at it, I was 25 at that time. It wasn't like today. I hadn't been travelling that much before that, and beside F2, which Fred put me in, he also put me in his Formula Atlantic team in America, so I was going backward and forward to America and Canada between the F2 races. I was exposed to the real Fred Opert, who was an extraordinary human being who mastered the art of travelling cheap, better than anyone in the world. He taught me so many things. I was just astonished."

Like Rosberg, Elgh was to experience Opert's penchant for minimising the cost of air travel.

"This was in the days when air tickets were just written with a pen, and Fred had in his briefcase about 50 different pens, ones with different blue and a different red. He had a pen for every occasion to match whatever had been written there before, to make it look like it was written by the same person. I tell you, I don't think I travelled once on a perfectly legal ticket, it was always a ticket on which he had managed to change the seven into an eight, or something like that.

"He also had his briefcase full of small stickers which the airlines used when you were able to change the ticket. You know, if you had a full fare ticket you were able to have the ticket changed. Fred had some contacts from every airline and he had a briefcase full of these small stickers so that even if the ticket was to Rome, somehow he managed to arrange a new sticker, and he would add a new date and a signature which looks like the one on the original ticket. That's the sort of thing that was going on."

Opert cultivated contacts at a number of airlines who were willing to ship all manner of race car components as 'hand luggage.'

"The thing was that Fred had a sponsorship arrangement with Goodyear. Goodyear [USA] gave him tyres, which I think were made for Formula Atlantic. They were called Blue Streak and they had a different profile. In order to save money, he insisted that we should run those tyres most times, which we did. And I never forget on those trips going back and forward to America and Europe, there was not one without me having to bring two or four tyres as hand luggage, which was supposedly not possible you know. Normally the instruction was, 'Okay, when you arrive at the airport there will be a blue van parked at this or this position, you go there. The name of the driver is such and such. You take him to the check-in,' – because I remember you could check in on the sidewalk – 'You go to number 22, there is a black guy named so and so. You say to him this is for Fred Opert Racing, you give him the tyres and he'll take care of it.'"

Motor racing always delivers highs and lows, and it was no different for Elgh when he was racing for Opert. At Long Beach he qualified on the front row, alongside pole man Bobby Rahal, and ahead of his teammate Keke Rosberg. He and Rahal tangled in the first corner, but despite that disappointment Elgh was delighted to have put a year-old car on the front row.

But Opert's relationship with Elgh was again put to the test at the Quebec street circuit.

"We had a race at Westwood in Vancouver that didn't go very well, then the following day we stayed on and went to another track, and I had a full day of testing – half a day in my car and half a day in Keke's car, which was a new car. I insisted that the new car was better. The problem was that Fred had no money and I knew he was struggling big time, but somehow, and this is just Fred, he heard what I said, and for the next race I had a new car.

109

"The next race was in Quebec City, a street race, and I remember that the car was not finished for first practice, it was only finished half way through the first qualifying. I remember they put the wheels on it and the car had never turned a wheel. I went like half a lap and I put the car in the wall trying to avoid a fast car coming from behind. I went too far off the line and there was stones and shit and I planted the car in the wall. It was the worst thing. I still have nightmares about it, because the walk back to the pits, to the garage, was very, very long. I never wanted to get back and face Fred because it was a big embarrassment.

"Somehow he always treated me as his son. The thing is, I had no money at all in those days. But I know that Keke was a different thing, Keke was more established and so on, and I know that Fred had problems to pay him and me. Even so, Fred gave me a company credit card and said, 'If you are stuck somewhere you can use it, but not otherwise.' It probably took me five minutes after he left, and I went and bought myself a new pair of shoes. But he was always very kind, very helpful. I had met my wife by that time and she came to some races and we were just like one big family and we were always travelling together – me, Keke, and my wife, and Fred, and Keke's girlfriend at the time. We had some fantastic times."

Elgh has a different recollection from Rosberg of Fred's racing activities in 1979, when he was briefly the team manager at the ill-fated ATS Formula One team.

"In '79, in parallel, he ran his Atlantic team and when he got stuck for drivers, or some sponsorship thing fell through, he called me. For example, he called me on a Wednesday night and said, 'You have to be in Montreal tomorrow because you have to race.'"

After 1979 Elgh started to race regularly in Japan, so there were long periods when the two men didn't meet up, but they continued to keep in contact by phone calls or letters. Once Elgh retired from racing he became a Formula One commentator, primarily on television.

Opert attended at least a couple of European Formula One races each year, which provided the opportunity for he and Elgh to meet up, and so over the last ten years of Opert's life there was once again regular contact. Fred visited Elgh's Spanish home and then, when the Elgh family moved back to Sweden, he visited them there.

"A few years ago, he came and stayed with us because he wanted to meet my grandchildren, and we always met around the world at the races."

Elgh visited Opert at his Ramsey home in New Jersey and at the Opert's holiday house at Martha's Vineyard.

"For Nico Rosberg's 20th birthday, I think it was his 20th birthday, we were all there – a fantastic week with Fred, but like I said, his health had been going down gradually. Many people thought that he had some sort of Parkinson's because he was always shaking. If you were having coffee with him, or having dinner, his hands were always shaking, but that [Parkinson's] was never his problem, he was like that when I first met him."

Elgh saw Opert's health decline, particularly in the last three years of his life. He was there to help his friend whenever he travelled to Europe, despite the difficulty of negotiating the increasingly restricted and professional world of Formula One. He discussed Opert's condition with Keke Rosberg and tried to convince Opert to be more realistic about his condition and his ability to travel and move around a Formula One paddock. But Opert was stubborn and motorsport was what he lived for, so Elgh's entreaties fell on deaf ears and he continued to look after him right up to his last F1 races in Hungary and Germany.

"Fred has been a very important part of my life, an important part of my career. He will never be forgotten by any of my family."

Opert retained most of his long-term friendships right up to the time of his death. He found time to keep in touch with friends, family and the surrogate family of young people who were important in his life.

12

Opert Reaches the Pinnacle of Motor Racing and the Depths of Disappointment

It seems natural that Opert would aspire to managing a Formula One team. There had been talk of him being involved in Formula One back in 1977 when Chevron owner, Derek Bennett, was working on an F1 design. Gossip favoured Opert to manage a Chevron F1 team, with Brian Hart engines, but Opert laughed at the idea, commenting that he and Chevron operated differently, and that 'the Bolton way of doing things' would have got in the way of a successful partnership. It seems more likely that Chevron manager Paul Owens would have expected to become the manager of any Chevron F1 team. Rivalry already existed between the Owens-managed factory F2 team and Fred Opert Racing. But it's interesting to imagine an Opert-managed Chevron F1 team, had Derek Bennett lived to complete his F1 car.

Opert had talked of a possible Formula One team during an interview with *The New York Times* in February 1978, but there is no way of knowing whether he was seriously considering this. However, he did speak about it when interviewed in '89, expressing regret that he hadn't taken the plunge to set up his own team.

"... there was a period where you could buy a Formula One car, you didn't have to produce it. That was the way to get in. I should've just skipped Formula Two and gone right into Formula One and found a sponsor, 'cause it's a lot easier to find a sponsor. Formula Two was really hard. It was expensive ..."

1979 was the year that the great motor racing partnership of Keke Rosberg and Fred Opert ceased, with Rosberg moving to racing in the Can-Am series and in Formula One. But the two were close friends and Rosberg had a hand in Opert's move into Formula One team management with ATS, which Opert related years later:

"At the end of the year Keke had done a couple of races for ATS, and everyone dreams when they get into Formula One it's going to be wonderful, but it was a disaster. I mean the cars were badly prepared, terrible mechanics. I was floundering around the end of '78, I didn't know what to do, and Keke liked Günter Schmid – one of the few people in the whole world that did – and he said [to Schmid], 'You know, here you've got this fucked up team and everything's going bad, bad mechanics. Why don't you hire Fred, 'cause all the best mechanics will work for Fred in a minute, and suddenly with Fred you'll get expertise, a well-run team that'll run on a tight budget, and with good mechanics, and end all your problems.' And Keke was right. He was 100 per cent right.

"I had no clue about ground effects when I arrived at ATS in January of '79 and I had to learn really, really fast. Our car worked, it took us a while because it was a piece of shit when I got there, but eventually, by the time I left we had a proper, really good, working car. When I left we probably had best skirts of any team. We were using parts off Canadian snowmobile runners, and our skirts worked really good. I had one man that I'd taken, and one French mechanic, actually, the fellow that worked on Prost's car in that one [F2] race, and I brought him to ATS, and I had one skirt man.

"If the guy [Schmid] had just left me to it, he would've had a decent Formula One team."

As it turned out it was an ill-fated move, as even the famous Fred Opert charm wasn't sufficient to build a relationship with the notoriously difficult German. Opert only lasted a few months at ATS before he resigned.

An article in *Autosport* magazine in 1979 reported Opert's resignation from ATS as follows:

"Following Günter Schmid's unfathomable decision to withdraw the car from the French Grand Prix (a move which hurt no one but ATS), Fred Opert has now resigned as team manager, and one can understand why."

Fred Opert was one of many casualties at ATS. Some of the sport's most experienced managers, including Jo Ramírez, Peter Collins and Alastair Caldwell were amongst the six managers that Schmid got through in four years.

David Williamson, who worked with Fred for three years, went to ATS when Fred became the team manager.

"It was a poisonous environment. It wasn't a pleasant experience. The only reason I stayed three weeks was because I got paid three weeks in advance."

Australian mechanic, Bernie Ferri, also went to ATS with Opert, and like Williamson he found it poisonous and left after the South American races. He recounts the unusual negotiations he had with Opert to get him to return to ATS for the South African Grand Prix.

"Fred got me to come back from Australia and then I went to Argentina and Brazil, for the Grand Prix, because he was team manager for ATS. I told Fred when I got back to England after that, I said, 'No, I'm sorry I can't hack this,' not the way it was. He said okay. I was lining up a job with Chaparral, they were fabricating the car in Luton. But Fred kept on at me, 'I've got no mechanics. You've left me in the lurch. You've got to go to South Africa.' I said, 'I'm not going to South Africa because on Monday I'm starting in Luton for Chaparral.' If they accepted me then I could go with the car to America. Fred said, 'No you've got to go,' and I said, 'No I'm not going.' Fred kept ringing and every time I'd say, 'I don't want to go.' Anyway, I had a whole pile of washing that needed to be done, so don't know what we got up to, but next time Fred rang I said, 'Right, first thing I do when I get there, I'm emptying my case and you'll get all my washing done,' and he said, 'That'll be fine.' So I flew to South Africa for two or three days just to get my washing done, and came back to London. That's what Fred was like. He thought that was really good. But ATS wasn't a nice place to be, that's why I got out of there."

After the disappointment of ATS, for the next two years Opert concentrated on his auto sales business. Then in 1983 he was lured back to the sport to run a Formula Atlantic car for his friend, Olivier Chandon. It proved to be a tragic decision.

Tragedy and the End of Motor Racing

I f Opert's week in prison was the first major turning point in his life, the death of his friend Olivier Chandon de Brailles, in March 1983, was the second. Chandon was 27 years old, the son of Frederic Chandon de Brailles, the Chairman of the Moët-Hennessy group.

When Chandon was killed in one of his cars, Opert walked away from motorsport.

Chandon lived in New York and became a friend of Opert's. He asked Opert to run a Formula Atlantic car for him, having previously raced in a Ralt RT5 Super Vee run by Wilbur Bunce Racing. Opert considered this to be the best funded venture of his management career.

"We had a jean company called Sasson Jeans and we had a budget of $332,000 – a third of a million dollars to run one car and a spare car in Atlantic. Everything to do it right ... and we were doing it right. We were down in January at Palm Beach and we had rented the track for four days, and mechanics, and he had an accident and drowned ... That year I had the right sponsor. I don't know how good a driver he would have been. He was more a personal friend than someone I discovered, and he did most of the work finding the sponsor, because he was French and these people that owned the jean company were French."

When he was testing a Ralt Formula Atlantic car at Moroso Motorsports Park (now Palm Beach International Raceway) in Florida, preparing for the WCAR Formula Atlantic (Mondial) Championship that would start in April, Chandon crashed and ended up upside down in a canal where he drowned. The roll bar sank into the mud, and it was impossible to get him out. Opert was devastated:

"In ten years of racing we never had anyone break a little finger," Opert said in an interview five years later. "His car flipped upside down into a canal, and he was drowned before we could get him out."

Considering how dangerous motor racing was in the period Opert was involved, it is remarkable that none of his drivers had been killed. But despite his comment about no one breaking even a little finger, there were injuries over the years, including Keke Rosberg who had a big accident at Saint-Fèlicien, in Canada, and was hospitalised. But no one suffered career- or life-threatening injuries.

Long-time Opert employee Linda Graham had to make the travel arrangements to Paris for the funeral, including for Chandon's girlfriend, Christie Brinkley. She remembers the impact that the accident had on Opert.

"That was it. He was done. He was done with racing at that point. He was finished."

After the funeral, Chandon's father flew to the States and Opert had the difficult task of taking him to the track so he could see where his son had been killed.

Opert's sister, Judi Sandler, believes that the death of Chandon was life-changing for her brother.

"After ATS Fred left racing, but then Chandon approached him to run a team. That [Chandon's death] was life changing for Freddie. Freddie was never an emotional person, but he was devastated by Chandon's drowning. Freddie took Olivier back to France on the Concorde. Had it been a race, there would have been stewards there to save him."

Opert's friend, Nikolai Koza, expressed the same view as Opert's sister.

"I think after Olivier died he really did not have the desire anymore. Not being able to save Olivier really was hard on him. Olivier had flipped his car at a test at Palm Beach Raceway. He was upside down in a swamp and Fred could not unbuckle him, despite his best efforts. After that he quit racing.

"Olivier was dating the swimsuit model Christie Brinkley at that time, or the actress Andie MacDowell. Either way Fred was close with both girls and accompanied them to the funeral."

Brian Robertson, who was previously Opert's partner in their Canadian business, was now the Ralt dealer and had sold Chandon's car to Opert. Robertson believes that Christie Brinkley was the source of the sponsorship for Chandon's Formula Atlantic series plans.

Opert's close friend and sometime business collaborator, Andreas Mann, also witnessed the impact of the tragedy on Opert.

"There was a big change in his life in 1983 when Chandon was killed. This was a point in his life that changed things completely."

Mark Coughlin went to work for Opert not long after Chandon had been killed.

"That was basically the thing, you know, that drove him to stop the race car dealing. He had that trailer that Valvoline had bought him, and he had another one, and they were all filled with cars and parts up at this house that he had up in Suffern, New York. It was just like he just stopped, and the trailers just sat there for a couple of years. It wasn't until somebody remembered that, 'Hey Fred probably has a lot of parts,' and started calling, he would send me up there to the damn trailer, and I'd start sifting through everything to try and find the parts that people were looking for.

"He just moved on from that chapter, which was interesting to me. He kept in touch with racing friends, but in that mid '80s period he really wasn't going to races as far as I know. He kept in touch with people and he would sell [road] cars to them, but he wasn't really active in racing. I think that it was just that it took the wind out of his sails with that loss ... It wasn't something that he dwelled on or anything, but I do recall him saying, 'That was it for me in racing after that happened.'"

Opert gave Coughlin the task of dealing with the disposal of the racing cars and parts. He didn't want anything to do with the business that had emotionally scarred him.

Life Beyond Motor Racing

After Chandon was killed, Opert turned all his attention to his business of exporting and importing road cars. A specialist area was the import of grey market cars that he would 'federalize' for legal sale in the USA.

Opert did business with a company called dp Motorsport E Zimmermann of Overath, Germany, for which he was the importer of its Porsches for North America. Staying with Porsche, Opert then got involved with Strosek Auto Design, a company founded by Vittorio Strosek, who had worked for Willy König before setting up on his own. Opert became the North America importer for Strosek, and did very well with it and dp Motorsport.

Opert was the only Strosek dealer in the USA. These special Porsches appealed to wealthy professional athletes, to whom Opert sold many cars, particularly baseball players. Some of these customers became good friends with Opert, including Manny Ramírez of the Cleveland Indians.

Mark Coughlin worked for Opert for two-and-a-half years, joining him the year after Olivier Chandon's tragic death.

Coughlin was still in high school when he first met Opert in 1975. He used to hang out at Opert's shop, and a friend of his bought a car from Barry Green, who was working for Opert at the time. Coughlin went to work for Apple initially, although retained his motoring interest by racing in Formula Ford and Sports 2000.

Coughlin wanted to buy a grey market Porsche from Opert. At the time, Opert had a lot of race car parts, gearboxes, and some race cars left over from his time in motorsport. He asked Coughlin, "Do you know anyone who needs these parts?" Coughlin got to know Opert, and after a while he went to work for him importing road cars and selling his race car parts.

"We would go over to the Frankfurt show and literally buy cars off the floor at the auto show. We'd drive them over to Bremerhaven and put them on a boat to send them back across to the States. We bought a bunch of four Porsche Turbos, we bought a Kremer K3. We bought a bunch of cars that you just couldn't get in the States.

"Fred had a telex in the office – which was the way you would communicate – and he had a guy, Klaus Bischof, who was in Cologne, who helped us find and broker cars all the time. I would work the Telex machine, sending all the option codes of cars that we were trying to get for people, whether they be Mercedes, BMW or Porsches. I went over to Europe two or three times on different buying expeditions. Fred would set up an itinerary for me to go to Kramer, and go to dp, and go over to Stuttgart, and then over to the M factory at BMW. He kept his fingers in a lot of places and, as it happens, guys who he had met through racing eventually moved into other areas of the business and, you know, he still kept in touch with folks.

"Then he started doing reverse deals, he was sending a lot of American cars to the Emirates and Saudi Arabia and those kinds of places. He was always working an angle and working a deal.

"He made a point of keeping in touch. It wasn't a case of just calling for something, he would just check in and see how people were doing, and he was always looking after people."

Opert surprised Coughlin when he took him to the famous Limelight nightclub in New York. Studio 54 and the Limelight were the two most famous disco clubs, and Opert frequented both. Studio 54 was known for its celebrity guest list that included the likes of Andy Warhol, Elizabeth Taylor, Truman Capote, and Woody Allen. Opert was a regular and seemed to know just about everyone there.

"I never had him down as this big club guy, but everybody and his brother knew Fred when he went to the Limelight. He was kind of a closet club guy, he didn't start happening until after midnight and then he'd be back at the shop the next morning by 8:30 or nine o'clock like nothing ever happened, and then do it again the next night, and the next night. He didn't drink but he made sure everybody else's glass was full and they were having a good time."

Opert did have an abrasive side which, like others who worked for him, Coughlin experienced from time to time.

"He called me an idiot plenty of times. He didn't suffer fools gladly, I'd say. And he would have his frustrations. He would get all keyed up about stuff, and the last thing you should tell Fred is to calm down when he is all keyed up about something. That would really flip him off. But he would always come back and invariably apologise for losing his cool, and that's fine by me because if you are going to be a jerk, but at least you realise you have been a jerk and apologise, that's fine."

After Coughlin left Opert in '87 he worked for Skip Barber before joining Opert's long-time sponsor, Valvoline. So things came full circle, as Coughlin ran the racing department at Valvoline for 12 years. Opert would call Coughlin to catch up or get passes to events, and they always kept in touch. Coughlin became very involved in IndyCar racing with Valvoline, and recounts how everywhere he turned he seemed to be dealing with people who had worked, or driven, for Opert.

"Barry Green ended up being the manager of the team that Valvoline supported in IndyCar racing. Then there was Bobby Rahal and Al Unser Jr. You know, it was like all these Fred alumni were kind of all around us. And then I worked with the Sports Car Club of America, and the guy that was President for a long time, Nick Craw, was also a guy that drove for Fred in Formula B. So, it's kind of the alumni group of Fred. It was him and Carl Hass that were importing all the cars back in the day. So he ran an awful lot of people and did a lot of wheeling and dealing."

John Leotta joined Opert a year or so after Coughlin left, and worked for him for 11 years, from 1989 to 2000. He joined him in the business on North Central Avenue, Ramsey in New Jersey.

When Leotta joined him, Opert was 50 years old and grey market cars had become a mainstay of his business. According to Leotta, Opert became "probably the biggest grey market dealer in the country."

Leotta tells the story of how he came to work for Opert.

"I came to him because I had read different articles about Fred and Fred Opert Racing. At the time I was detailing high-end cars, so when I saw that he had moved close to where I was living, I went to him. He was a hard person to deal with because he didn't like cold calls, he didn't like people walking in and saying, 'Hey, this is my business and I can help you.' So I made him a deal, I said, 'Give me the worst car you have and I will detail it for free, and if you are happy we will do business.'

"He has told a couple of people over the years that he was very impressed when I walked in and did that for him. And that kind of started things off.

"He would be away for a week or ten days and it was just the two of us; he had a book keeper, but she worked in a different location, so I was the go-to guy. We were very different, so a lot of people, I think, liked to deal with me, because sometimes Fred was harsh. When it was business, that's what it was: business. He didn't want to chit chat or anything, just do the deal and that's it."

Opert recognised an opportunity to exploit the tourist delivery programs of the European luxury car manufacturers, particularly Porsche, BMW, Volvo, Audi and Mercedes. This program allowed a buyer to order a car then take delivery from the factory. The manufacturer would include a factory tour, or some other interesting activity, plus a night in a top hotel, before handing the keys over to the new owner. The owner could then drive the car before having it shipped back to their home country. Opert realised that this was a cost-effective way of importing new luxury vehicles into the USA. He bought cars in the names of friends and family then flew someone to Europe to collect the car.

Continued on page 129

Rosberg, Opert and Dick Bennetts in New Zealand 1977. (Courtesy Terry Marshall)

Opert and Bobby Rahal, New Zealand, 1978. (Courtesy Terry Marshall)

1 *Rosberg in action at the Manfeild circuit in New Zealand's North Island. (Courtesy Ross Cammick)*

2 *Rosberg and Opert in Canada in 1978. (Courtesy Opert family)*

3 *Opert's sister-in-law, Stephanie, Rosberg, and Opert at Monaco in 1981. Rosberg doesn't look too concerned that he failed to qualify the Fittipaldi. (Courtesy Opert family)*

Opert's dream of running an F1 team became a nightmare.

Opert with the victorious Keke Rosberg at Wigram, New Zealand.

Opert and his good friend Bobby Brown at Brown's 50th in 1990. (Courtesy Bobby Brown)

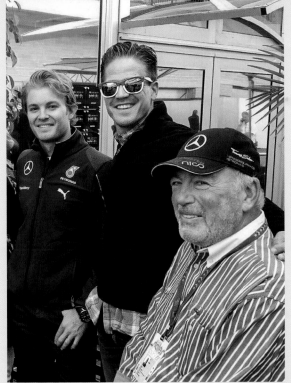

Nico Rosberg, Nikolai Koza (Kozarowitzky) and Fred Opert. (Courtesy Nikolai Koza)

Nikolai Koza and Opert at the
Austin Grand Prix in 2015.
(Courtesy Nikolai Koza)

Opert's pass for the last GP he
attended – Hungarian GP in
2016.

Opert's nephew, Derek, became something of a tourist delivery courier, as he flew to Germany on several occasions to collect a new car, enjoy being spoilt by the manufacturer, then deliver the car to its shipping point for its trip to the USA and Opert's dealership.

"He sent me to Germany six or seven different times where I would go to pick up a car. He would pay me to fly over there. I'd go to Mercedes, I'd go to BMW, and pick up cars, and I'd drive them round for a few days and I'd ship them back to him. He'd already purchased them for a buyer, but it was cheaper for him to do it this way.

"Mercedes did it, BMW did it, Audi did it. If you bought the car, you got to go over to the country, pick up the car, drive it out the door of the factory, drop it off to one of their shipping stations anywhere throughout Europe, and then it would come back in a month or so.

"Mercedes would put you up for two nights in a five-star hotel from a list of hotels in Europe. Audi would have a limousine driver pick you up at the airport and drive you to Ingolstadt and put you up for a night in a hotel there. I picked up cars from every city. I did it all by myself when I was in college."

Nikolai Koza was also involved in Opert's tourist delivery purchases, often unwittingly.

"All of a sudden I would get in the mail, 'Thank you for buying this Porsche,' or 'Thank you for buying this BMW,' or Audi, and I'd say 'What is this?' And he [Fred]'d say, 'Yeah, yeah, I just put your name on it. I just had to put somebody's name on it to buy this car.' And I'm like, 'Yeah Fred, but I hope I'm not getting in any trouble here.' And he'd say, 'No, no. Don't worry about it.' So, for years I'm getting this mail, like I've been buying all these cars."

John Leotta believes that they were doing more tourist delivery BMWs than any BMW dealer in the world.

"... which is kind of interesting, because there was just the two of us. Fred was very switched on with that. Fred was a very crafty, intelligent person."

Leotta was another of Opert's tourist delivery couriers making regular trips to Europe, to the point where he was well known at the BMW and Porsche factories. Opert also had a colleague in Germany, his good friend Andreas Mann, who was able to help out with any local arrangements.

Opert was a good organiser, who always had numerous deals on the go, and was able to keep many balls in the air. Leotta saw this first hand over the years.

"I always said that Fred would have been brilliant as a manager for maybe The Rolling Stones, or some hugely popular band. Fred was extremely intelligent. I don't know if the word 'ruthless' is too harsh, but he really was very assertive, and he pushed me with a lot of things."

Opert had a sense of humour as well as being very creative, and Leotta enjoyed many laughs as he witnessed Opert in action.

"Before we got the internet, all of his advertising was always very unique in his wording. He was very creative with *The New York Times* and various publications for advertising cars.

"I remember in *The New York Times* ... The girls, when they were taking the ads on the line, they didn't understand what 'wanker' was and he would always put 'No wankers apply.' Because we were selling expensive cars we would get all these morons and very strange people, so he would always figure out a way to sneak in 'No wankers apply.'

"Being that he was doing business all around the world, and this is pre-cell phones, everybody around the world I guess knows Mickey Mouse. So he got his phone in Ramsey listed under Mickey Mouse. He put it under M Mouse. And I remember when he spoke to the phone company, obviously they would have thought it was a joke if he said 'I want to put it under Mickey Mouse,' so he said his aunt would be living in the house and her name was M Mouse [pronounced Moos], then spelled it out M O U S E."

No doubt Opert simply told people to call Mickey Mouse if they wanted to get in touch with him. That would be a lot easier than carrying business cards, or writing down a phone number.

"I always found it amazing. We would get mail that literally only said [was addressed] Fred, or Fred Opert Racing, USA. That's it, nothing else in the address – no zip code, no town, no street, and it would find its way to Fred. He was definitely a unique character, that's for sure. He lived to the beat of his own drum.

"He was very creative with his travel. Nowadays I don't think anybody could do what he did with the airlines. This was pre-personal computers and the internet. He would do these extremely strange deals where he would buy a one-way ticket somewhere and then get a round trip ticket from there, he would spend hours on the phone and he would figure out all these ways of how to manipulate the system and save money. It was funny but, you know, it worked."

Sadly, after 11 years together Leotta left when Opert reneged on an agreement he had made with him.

"In 1992 Fred came to me and said he was planning on retiring in the year 2000, and, since he had no children, he would be giving me the business. This was very exciting to me, and I took it very seriously and worked very hard. Fred came to me in November 1999 and told me that he had changed his mind and would not be leaving the business, and that if I wanted to stay on I was welcome to. I decided to leave the business."

This seems out of character for Opert who prided himself on doing deals on a hand shake. He also held others to their word, believing that a deal was a deal once someone made a commitment, even if it was only verbal.

Nikolai Koza tells a story that underscores Opert's view that when someone made a commitment he expected them to honour it.

"Fred and I are in Austin at the F1 race, and Fred had made a deal with Ron Dennis a couple of years prior when McLaren was still winning. Lewis was driving. Ron said, 'Well it seems Fred, every time you are here, we're winning.' And Ron told him, 'Every time we win and you're here Fred, I'm picking up your expenses.' And Fred took that seriously, because (I think it was 2013 or '14) he said, 'Nikolai I've got to go and see Ron; I've got to give Ron this invoice.' And he tells me the story and I said, 'Are you serious?' But Fred was bloody serious, so we sat down with Ron, and Fred had to remind Ron about the deal. I think it was 13 or 14 thousand dollars eventually. And Ron was completely taken aback, and I handed the invoice over to Ron, and I'm sitting there, and Ron didn't know what to do. But he said, 'Fair's fair. I'll take care of it.' Fred would hold people to things, no matter who it was. No matter how big Ron had got over the years, Fred would still hold people accountable. Ron was really baffled. It was really funny."

So perhaps as the year 2000 approached, he – like many men facing retirement – simply couldn't deal with the pending void; a life without wheeling and dealing. He had found it hard enough to attend motor races simply as a spectator without any function; even when he attended Grands Prix to follow the career of Nico Rosberg it's likely that he saw himself there as a mentor and advisor. He would not have been content to sit in the sun at Martha's Vineyard, or in Florida, reading *Road & Track* magazine.

Opert exported cars as well as importing them. His friend, and ex-driver, Bobby Brown was involved in providing cars for export.

"I sold him a lot of Chevrolets that he was exporting to Switzerland and Brazil, but then GM got ticked off and tightened up. I think Fred made a fair amount of money doing it through the '70s and '80s.

"I know he was doing deals and sending cars to Brazil right to the end, mainly SUVs. He had a small showroom and he would buy and sell specific cars. He had a deal with the modified Porsche people. He had deals in Europe because he was over there. He was a savvy business guy. He didn't live an extravagant life. His extravagance was his travel to F1 or to see me in Brazil."

One of Opert's more enterprising schemes was to export the new retro VW Beetles to Germany in the late '90s. After the new Beetle's introduction into the USA, there were long waiting lists of people back in Germany wanting to buy these cars. Opert saw this as an opportunity and, with the help of his brother, bought new and used cars from USA dealers. He then sold them to German buyers and exported them back to Germany, referring to them as "swimmers," as he thought of them as swimming back home.

Opert never did retire, and was doing business right up to the time of his death. His German friend, Andreas Mann – who often helped him with the logistics of exporting cars from Europe to the USA, and importing from the USA – remembers that in the weeks just before he died, for the first time, Opert missed some of the details of a deal.

"Fred always had his way and he always had his timing. He was always perfectly organised. He set the standard very high. But when I picked up a car four weeks before he died it was the only time that everything was not completely organised."

The Surrogate Family

Fred Opert didn't have children of his own. After his five-year marriage to Sharon Scheibelhut he didn't remarry, but he had an ability to connect with young people, and he effectively created a surrogate family of the sons, and a daughter, of his friends and siblings. The relationship between Opert and this surrogate family reveals a lot about the man – his desire to influence their lives so that they didn't settle for mediocrity; his conviction that his ideas were right and should be adopted; and his compulsion to micro-manage, albeit with the best of intentions. These were the traits that sometimes drove them crazy, but that they mostly appreciated in a man they loved.

Opert remained friends with a number of drivers who drove for him, including the Finn Mikko Kozarowitzky. Kozarowitzky and Keke Rosberg went to New Zealand with Opert for the 1977 Peter Stuyvesant Series. Rosberg won that championship, and as his star started to rise Kozarowitzky's started to fade. After a couple of ill-fated efforts in Formula One he was unable to secure a full-time role as a driver. In the years that followed Opert became close to Kozarowitzky's son, Nikolai, and when things were not going well for Nikolai at home, he left Finland and flew to New York. Keke Rosberg summed up the situation:

"He [Fred] was, in his way, the big family man, you know. In the same way that Kozarowitzky's son now lives in New York. He didn't land there by accident; he landed there because 'Uncle' Fred was there. He was also one of the best friends of Fred, although a different generation. Fred was the godfather for all our kids. He was not the actual godfather, but he behaved like one. He behaved like all godfathers should behave."

It was as if Opert missed not having a son, so he 'adopted' the sons of friends and family – of Mikko Kozarowitzky and Keke Rosberg – and Opert's own nephew Derek (the son of his brother Larry). These young men were friends who kept in touch and, along with Lauren, his sister's daughter, they became Opert's surrogate family.

Derek Opert is quite clear about his view of his uncle's 'adopted' family:

"Fred had three sons: Me, Nico and Nikolai."

Nikolai Koza (having shortened his name from Kozarowitzky) lived at Opert's home in New York in 1996. He had known Opert since he was four or five years old, as Opert had made frequent visits to the Kozarowitzky home when he visited Europe. Back in 1992, Nikolai had spent the summer with him, washing cars at the Opert business in New Jersey.

"He had the car dealership. I had a really nice time. All I did was wash cars and went around with Fred, and had a really good time. Fred suggested I should do my senior year in high school in the US in '96 and I could live at his place, which I did."

So, in 1996 Nikolai returned to the USA and lived with Opert while he studied.

"I went to school where he lived in Ramsey, New Jersey. Fred was an interesting guy to live with. He was very methodical. He was not very emotional, but I always knew he cared in a way. He was like a father figure because my dad ended up on the wrong side of the tracks. Fred was always there for me. Fred never had kids, but he always had a very close relationship with me and of course Derek, his only nephew.

"You know, Fred was always on top of my grades. He made sure I had a good regime of doing my study and my sports, but at the same time making sure I had a car to wash every day after school. He never let me leave without $20 in my pocket. He cared about my grades, if it wasn't an 'A' he would be very disappointed, and I'd say, 'Why do you care? You're not my dad.' But he did care and that was nice."

Nikolai was also a racer and he raced in the United States during 1996 in Formula Ford 2000 races. Opert took Nikolai to the tracks and introduced him to a lot of racing people.

"Fred did help me in racing, he helped pay for the Skip Barber racing series in 1996, as well as the Bertil Roos racing series which I did first after karting. I always had the Fred Opert logos on my suit and car, but I raced for other teams."

Opert was a very sound sleeper and a notoriously loud snorer, a combination that contributed to Nikolai suffering a serious injury during a race meeting in Miami, probably through a lack of sleep.

"When I was racing in Miami once, Fred had sent me there by myself and he came to join me. And you know, Fred would snore so bad, it was horrible. He said, 'We'll share the hotel room,' and I'm thinking, 'Oh, please no.' We were in the Miami Homestead and I remember the first night he falls asleep instantly. And he starts snoring and I can't sleep, and I'm trying to push him and roll him over, but he just won't wake up. I thought, 'I'll sleep in the bath tub,' but I could still hear him from the bathroom. So eventually I just crawled into the back of our little Dodge Neon rental. And I slept in the back of that car for three nights.

"I ended up breaking my neck in one of the races there. I don't blame Fred for it, but I had a really bad accident and I totalled the car – all four wheels off, the engine broke off the chassis. I had an initial check-up and the doctors said it felt good, but I had a lot of pain in my neck, and they took an X Ray, but from the wrong angle. Fred was saying, 'He's fine, he's fine.' When I came back to Europe I had an MRI and they said, 'Well, you definitely broke your neck.' I was very lucky. It wasn't a bad fracture, but it was a fracture. To this day I still have issues with it."

Despite the difference in their ages Nikolai and Fred got on well. Opert had a busy social life in which he included Nikolai.

"Fred would go to Studio 54 in New York city and party with all the celebrities. I was a young guy, and Fred took me to the Playboy Awards of the Year in New York and I have some funny pictures with me and the playmates.

"He was funny – I remember when I got my first fake ID and he said, 'Well let's go and try it.' And we went to this bar that had a singles night. I was barely 17, and the guy instantly knew that my ID was fake, and Fred and I had to run out of there. But many times we would go to the city and he would say, 'Come on, let's go out.' He was a women's man, he would always go after the ladies. He would always try to set me up and double date and I'd say, 'Fred you're 60.'

"He had a way of conning the women and it was funny. He wasn't a good-looking guy with his belly, and he was bald. But Fred was a playboy."

Despite the famous Opert smile and natural warmth, there was an abrasive side to the man that Nikolai saw during his time with him.

"He didn't have very good people skills, I think. He was very kind to people and to his clients. He sold cars all over the world, to athletes, specifically American athletes, and baseball and basketball players, and he would always make sure that we got tickets to events, and he got very close to some of the biggest baseball stars in the US, and became personal friends with these people.

"On the other side he would not hesitate to call somebody stupid or retarded. You couldn't take things too personal. But you know John Leota [who worked for Opert for 11 years] takes things much more personal, but Fred would say 'Are you stupid?' That would make it very tough on John, and that was a side that if you didn't know Fred you had a hard time living with it, but I never really had that issue with him."

Fred and Nikolai had a lot of fun together with cars, aside from the racing.

"Every time he would buy a new car he would always go with me to see if the zero to 60 mile-an-hour time was accurate. We would go on the turnpike and I would have to sit with my analogue stopwatch and measure for him.

"I wasn't allowed to have a license back then. There was something with my visa and they couldn't therefore issue me with a social pin number, but Fred would always let me drive cars. I remember one time we drove with walkie talkies to Martha's Vineyard. I didn't have a license and I was following in this car to bring it up to his sister's house on Cape Cod. He didn't really care too much about the law on some occasions, and any time he could save a buck on taxes he'd always try."

After his year in high school, in 1996, Nikolai went back to racing in Europe and did his college studies in the Netherlands. In 2002 he returned to the USA again, intending to race in the Formula Atlantic series. Nikolai and Fred hadn't been in contact as often during Nikolai's time in the Netherlands, after Opert cut off contact with Nikolai's father, but when Nikolai returned to the USA in 2002 the pair reconnected. Nikolai's racing plans foundered after he lost his German manager and his sponsorship, so he travelled the USA with friends, and lived in California for a time.

He ended up back in New York, short of money, and with the intention of returning home. However, then he met his wife to be and, as he put it, "had to find a real job." He had to wait eight months for a visa. It was very hard to get work but Opert helped out as much as he could.

"Fred was very kind, any time he had a job he would always call me. I would go over to his house and do his lawn or paint his house. Do all different kind of things. Then Fred got very close over the years with my two daughters. They were really, really sad when he passed away because he was always very kind to them. He would remember birthdays and Christmas. He took a big interest in my kids.

"He was always thinking about my daughter and how to get her more involved in racing, because she raced go-karts. But after I got divorced the budget constraints became tighter. Fred was always trying to think about Victoria, but it was not meant to be, and that's alright, but he really cared a lot.

"I loved Fred like a father. He was an amazing guy and I feel very privileged to have had him in my life. I miss him a lot."

Derek Opert, Fred's nephew, became another of the trio of surrogate sons.

Through his uncle, Derek met and became friends with Nikolai. Nikolai and Derek met for the first time in 1992, the first summer that Nikolai stayed with Opert, when Opert and Nikolai went up to Cape Cod for Nikolai's birthday. Derek's parents, Larry and Stephanie, were also there.

Fred was giving Derek motorised cars when he was only three or four years old, and as Derek got older Fred started to make some moves to interest the boy in motorsport. He bought Derek a go-kart, which Derek tested alongside Nikolai. However Derek's parents had seen the tragedy that the sport can bring when Olivier Chandon was killed in one of Opert's cars just a year before Derek was born. When they found out that their son had be secretly testing a kart they put a stop to it.

"We tested it in the empty parking lot of an industrial factory in New Jersey on a Sunday when nobody was there. My parents found out after that first time and put an end to it.

"He had bought me a Bell racing helmet right before that as well. I still have the helmet, and it currently sits on a mantle next to Fred's racing helmet from his racing days, which I got after he passed away."

"There was always tension between my Dad and Fred I think, from before I was even born.

"My parents were extremely close with him back when he had a racing team. My parents would go and spend a month in Europe every year with him, staying in Saint-Tropez driving around to different places. One year, before I was born, there was a fall out about a restaurant choice in Saint Tropez. So, when I was born I would describe the situation as friendly but not close."

Fred Opert always wanted to be in control and the falling out between he and his brother, Larry, was simply about a choice of restaurant; Fred had suggested to Larry that they should go to a particular restaurant one night. Larry said he would run it by Stephanie, but Fred scoffed at that and went ahead and booked the restaurant.

"I think there was some resentment from my dad towards Fred, because Fred was trying to treat me like a kid of his own in pushing me towards racing. When he bought me a go-kart that was a big issue ... having me go to New York to practice it without them knowing."

Opert's protégé and good friend Keke Rosberg has a son, Nico, a similar age to Derek. Nico had started to follow in his world champion father's footsteps and was racing go-karts. Perhaps Opert was influenced by this, and as he didn't have a son of his own simply substituted his nephew as the son he would have encouraged to take up motor racing, as Nico Rosberg had.

The fact that Derek didn't go on to race didn't stop him becoming Opert's motorsport buddy. At the age of 12 Derek went to an IndyCar race with Opert, as a guest of Barry Green, who had once worked for Opert but by then was a successful IndyCar team owner. Derek still remembers his uncle buying him a Marlboro Team Penske hat.

In 2000, when he was 16, Derek attended his first Formula One race in Montreal. Despite his young years Derek got permission from his parents to catch a bus to Montreal from Boston. Opert, who had driven from New York, picked him up at the bus station. Derek remembers meeting Johnny Herbert, who was driving for Jaguar; Mika Häkkinen; and Jean Todt, who was General Manager of Ferrari at the time. The day after the race Opert dropped his nephew back at the bus station in the morning, even though the bus to Boston wasn't leaving until late in the day. Derek went to see the movie *Shaft* to kill some time, not realising that, because he was in Montreal, it was in French.

These early trips to race meetings planted the seeds of a friendship between Derek and his uncle, based around motorsport, that lasted until Opert's death in 2016.

When Derek was in college, in his teenage years, the friendship became stronger and the two men became closer, talking regularly on the phone.

In 2006 Derek was studying in Aix-en-Provence, in France, as his father Larry had done before him. Fred planned to attend the F1 race in Monaco and take Derek with him. It was Nico Rosberg's first year in F1, racing for the Williams team, and he had made a brilliant debut in his first race in Bahrain, where he had come from dead last after a pit stop to drive through to seventh place and set the fastest lap. Even Sir Jackie Stewart was impressed.

"I think it's the best performance of any young driver that I've seen for a very long time," the three-time world champion said.

"I can't remember a performance in a first Grand Prix that was so impressive. I had a sixth place in my first Grand Prix, but he came from the back and I certainly didn't get fastest lap. His judgement, the manner in which he went about it ... it's a rare commodity today, but as a racing driver he knows how to pass and carries it out."

Opert was following Nico's career with even more fervour, as Derek reports:

"I used to get weekly clippings in the mail about Nico from Fred, and he would call me after every F1 practice and race to discuss what had happened in detail."

Opert wanted to see Nico race at Monaco and have Derek meet him. Derek says that getting a paddock pass for Monaco was nigh-on impossible, but Fred wrote a long letter to Bernie Ecclestone telling him that Derek and Nico Rosberg were close friends (they had yet to meet) and that Derek lived in France. There were further embellishments, but they did the trick and they were granted their paddock passes.

"I took the train to Monaco and met him at the track. We went to qualifying."

But all did not go smoothly. The previous year, when Fred was leaving his hotel, he commented to the desk staff that he liked the room and asked if he could have it the following year. The proprietor said yes, and Fred, being an old-school person, assumed that a deal had been done and didn't follow up with any confirmation or payment; he simply turned up and was stunned to hear that the hotel was fully booked, including 'his' room. Uncle and nephew then went on a futile hunt for another room, but there was nothing to be had in the principality, so they ended up sharing a room in Nice where Derek got little sleep due to his uncle's notorious snoring.

"We had to drive around. This was before online existed where you could search for hotels. We went door-to-door to hotels, everything was booked, till finally we found this one hotel in Nice that had an empty room. It was a four- or five-star hotel right on the Promenade des Anglais that was, like, 500 a night, and we couldn't get two rooms for the next four days, so I ended up having to share a room with him.

"Fred was a big snorer, so I don't think I slept one night for four nights. But we went to the race. I met Nico for the first time and I met Keke Rosberg for the first time. Eje [Elgh] was actually a commentator for Swedish TV at that point, so I also met Eje for the first time. Eje gave us seats to sit in the stand, so Fred and I would go back and forth, although he was having trouble walking any distance at that point, or he didn't want to. It was a difficult thing to get him to go over to the seats."

After the race uncle and nephew went on to spend a week in Saint-Tropez together.

"He had a favourite club that he used to always take my parents to when they were in Saint-Tropez. He wanted to go there with me. This is my first night in Saint-Tropez. We walked in.

"Fred was one of those people who never realised how old he was or how overweight he was, he just thought he was still the same 30-year-old guy from when he raced. He walked into the bar and pointed to the two most attractive girls at the bar – mind you I'm 20 years old at the time – and he said, 'Alright, go talk to those two girls and then I'll come over.' He was dead serious.

"One of those things that you learn about Fred through life is that if he comes up with an idea you can't convince him otherwise, you are just better off doing it. So, you kinda have to suck up your pride and just do it, otherwise you'll never hear the end of it from him. So I did. It was definitely one of my more embarrassing experiences. He had that way about him.

"I remember going to one of the beach clubs in Saint-Tropez when we were there, and he had no problem seeing the most attractive girl lying out on the deck there, and he would just walk up and lie down next to her and start talking to her, and he thought there was nothing weird about it.

"Women loved him. He was a very generous person, he would always buy a drink or pick up an expensive tab and never think twice about it. He was extremely generous in that regard and just super friendly in a non-threatening way. I think younger women saw this charming – albeit bald and overweight – guy, who clearly had a swagger to him from his younger days. It was funny to watch."

Opert was determined that Derek should be involved in motorsport one way or another. After Derek finished college, on one of their trips to the Canadian Grand Prix in Montreal, Opert introduced him to team owner Frank Williams. Fred encouraged Derek to send his resume to Williams to get a job with the team. But Derek didn't believe that Frank Williams had shown any special interest, and he decided not to write to the team owner. Derek says that his uncle never let him forget that.

Fred and Derek went to the Grand Prix at Montreal each year, which is where Derek would catch up with Nico Rosberg. Derek experienced Fred's unusual priorities when it came to spending money.

"He was very generous with money, but at the same time the things he spent money on were always weird. He would stay at a cheapest hotel he could find in the French quarter in Montreal, where you're staying in a place where you don't even want to touch the bed sheets, because he didn't want to spend all the money on hotels ... or expensive ones, but then the next night you'd go out to dinner and he would pay for a $2000 dinner tab. It was one of those things that didn't reconcile.

"Fred was a difficult guy, but someone who I loved."

Opert was also determined that Derek and Nico Rosberg should be friends, and they did build a friendship even though their meetings were restricted to race meetings, primarily in Montreal. They shared their grief with a phone call after Opert died. Just a few months later Nico achieved his world championship and sent Derek a special book about his championship season.

Given the strong relationship between Fred Opert and Keke Rosberg it was inevitable that Opert would 'adopt' Nico Rosberg when he came on the scene.

Nico remembers Fred fondly.

"He has always been close to our family, and I always remember him as such an enthusiastic, very nice guy, and absolute racing fanatic; always telling the old stories about how it was with my dad back in the '70s where they had no money, no nothing, and yet they somehow managed to go racing and win races."

Nico's racing career became an important part of Fred's life, it provided his continuing link to Formula One. He coached Nico as he had coached his own drivers when he was running his teams. He wanted Nico to succeed.

"He was just a fan, you know, because I was the son of my dad. He really liked my dad back in the day. They had so much success together. So that's how it came about, and he was always very supportive.

"I even had to send him all my reports from all the races when I was go-karting. He requested them, and was always giving me advice on them because I was also sending them to Ron Dennis. He was really always there supporting and guiding me, he was a fan from day one really, and I'm very thankful for that support."

Opert's belief in Nico did waver briefly in 2016, when Nico relinquished his championship lead to Lewis Hamilton; Fred shared his doubts with his nephew, Derek.

"One of the last conversations I had [with Fred] – which is kind of sad to think about, because this is the year that Nico did win the championship when he [Fred] passed away – but Nico had just had a bad stretch and he said to me, 'I honestly just don't think that Nico has it, I don't think he has it in him to be a champion.' I mean he wanted it, and he was very active in his career."

No doubt unaware of Opert's comment Nico went on to win the championship that year. Nico recalls:

"Fred really was always one of my number one fans, so it was incredible he was always so excited to see me race. I remember that he said a driver's career goes in chapters ... one chapter was winning the first race, and there was a chapter for each important step, and I think we got to chapter 15 or something, by the time I was leading the championship in 2016."

Nico was surprised when Opert appeared in Hungary and then Germany in 2016, while he was fighting Lewis Hamilton for the championship.

"He even came to a race in 2016, although the doctors said he should not leave the hospital. He just disappeared on his own, travelled all the way across the Atlantic, nobody knows how he even made it because he could hardly walk any more at that time, so it was incredible. Such a pity that he didn't see the end result with me winning the championship. That's really regrettable."

Derek Opert described his uncle's ebullient support for Nico.

"He's followed Nico's entire career from when he was a young karter to the present, and he always wanted Nico to succeed and he liked being involved in the racing aspect.

"As years progressed, Nico was kind of his way to stay involved in racing, and stay active and be part of it.

"It was almost like coaching. He had coached so many great race car drivers in his early years that he would pick people like me and Nico to try to coach as well ... trying to propel him to be successful.

"I think his personal connection with Nico through Keke allowed him really to feel like he was involved. It almost allowed him to continue his coaching.

"It was never that he needed Nico to win the championship, he just wanted to be a part of it."

When asked about Opert's ability to relate with and be close to younger people like Nikolai, Derek and himself, Nico Rosberg answered simply.

"He was such a young and fun guy and speaks the youth language ... Yeah, we just always got on well."

Lauren – The Surrogate Kid Sister

If the three boys, Derek, Nikolai and Nico, were Fred's motor racing sons, his niece, Lauren, was his arts, music and movie 'kid sister.' Lauren Sandler is Fred's sister's daughter. She is an accomplished writer, with a number of books to her name and many articles, columns and opinion pieces published in leading USA publications. She has written regularly about women's issues, the politics of relationships, feminism, and conservative women's movements. This made for a robust and complicated relationship with her uncle, who she described as 'a bundle of contradictions.'

Lauren tells the story of her mother buying Fred a set of navy blue bath towels with a pig embroidered on them. Rather than being monogrammed with Opert's initials they were monogrammed with the letters MCP ... for Male Chauvinist Pig. The family was fond of a good joke and Lauren says that this was her mother's way of having a dig at Fred in a "deeply affectionate but deeply honest way." After Fred died, Lauren chose one of these towels as a memento of her uncle.

Lauren was born around the time that Fred and his wife Sharon (Sherri) split up. She came to consider Fred to be more of a big brother than an uncle. They both had a love of theatre, the arts, and music, with Bob Dylan, The Rolling Stones and The Clash being shared passions.

When Lauren was a child she lived with her parents in an apartment in Cambridge, Massachusetts. She didn't see a lot of her uncle there, but her grandparents had a place on Cape Cod where the whole family would spend weekends. Opert was keen to expose his niece to music and the arts, and would record cassette tapes of whatever he was listening to give to her.

"My first really deep cultural immersion with Fred was him buying records, on vinyl, many of which I now have – his original records – and making me Maxell cassette tapes of the Rolling Stones, or Rod Stewart, or Bob Dylan, and filling in all the different songs, etc, and bringing me these cassette tapes to my grandparents' house on Cape Cod. He would drive up from New Jersey on a Friday night. It would take most people probably six hours, it took him about four and a half. He'd get in about 2:30 in the morning, my grandmother would be waiting up scared to death, totally over-protective. And we would all spend the weekend together."

When Lauren was older she would stay with Opert at his place in New Jersey.

"He would love that. He would take me and a friend to go see a concert in New York city. He loved Reggae and Rock. And he loved the idea to take me to these things that he thought were super cool, and I did too. We would also travel with him quite a bit, there was often a summer trip in France or Italy, or a winter trip in Barbados or Saint Martin, and he was always looking for things that we could be doing. You know, I was always the youngest kid at a nightclub; if there was a good band playing or something like that, he just wanted me to hear them. I think that he wanted to introduce me to that, but I also think that we were good companions throughout it.

"He got me a subscription to *Rolling Stone* magazine when I was ten or 12 and kept it going until I was in college. These were just parts of how we were close. And then I moved to New York for college. I went to Colombia University and during that time he would appear and take me to the theatre. He really loved this one theatre called the Atlantic Theatre Company in Chelsea. The playwright David Mamet was a founder of this theatre and Freddie just loved David Mamet plays. Sort of like, aggressive, '80s, male ... you know. I loved those too. So he got into that and then he would become obsessed with Martin Scorsese movies and he would call me up after he saw every new Scorsese movie, or after he saw every episode of *The Sopranos*. You know, he could really talk on the phone. That was another way that we connected around all of this stuff."

In the mid-1970s Lauren's parents built a house at Martha's Vineyard, which became the new gathering place for the family. Fred had his own room in that house which everyone referred to as 'Fred's Room.' They decorated it with pictures of

France. He loved the place and added two framed posters, one of the writer William Faulkner, the other of Saint-Tropez. He had his own stool at the bench in the kitchen, next to the phone, where he'd sit with his laptop on the bench while he monopolised the phone.

Opert had a desire to expose people, particularly the young people in his life, to the things that interested him and that he thought they should take in interest in. He had very specific ideas about the way he thought people's lives could be shaped if they were only ambitious enough – or determined enough, or had the right priorities, or the right connections – but he also had very specific ideas about how things could be done. When he had an idea, that idea was the thing that mattered.

"If it wasn't Freddie's idea, it just wasn't going to matter as much. And if it was Fred's idea, then you'd better do it. This is why he was so infuriating."

He could be unrelenting, convinced that his ideas were right and so important that other people should take note of them. Some found this overpowering, but others accepted that 'that was Fred,' and could quietly make fun of his obsession. He was dogged in telling people what he thought they should be doing and how they should do it.

"He had certain ways of thinking about things and he wanted you to pay attention. We used to joke that you would talk to Freddie on the phone and he'd be telling you something, and he'd command you to 'get a pen.' Because he believed that what he had to say was so important that it must be written down. And it was always about something that he thought you should be doing.

"There are a couple of stores that we have seen around the world that are called, 'Get a Pen.' They sell really nice pens and we always took pictures of ourselves in front of the Get a Pen stores and joke about Freddie. He would be insisting on something that you should be doing with your car, with your career. It was usually unsolicited. It was often out of the context of one's own reality but, God damn it, you can listen to it.

"He'd get in your car, you'd have the wrong floor mats and he suggested that you should get a different type of floor mat. He just couldn't get over it. He would note it and he would get a big smile on his face like, 'how could you do that?' smile. And he would go on and on and on about why this small choice, or big choice, or whatever it was, wasn't just wrong, but was absolutely unthinkably wrong. And that's how he would approach a lot of things. That's how he would approach political arguments … or salad dressing."

When Lauren finished college in 1996 she worked as a producer for National Public Radio in Washington. After a few years she returned to New York and went to graduate school, then became a writer. She was a regular contributor to a number of women's magazines, including *Marie Claire*. Her uncle was convinced that she should write a profile on Nico Rosberg for *Marie Claire*. The pair had an on-going argument about this over many years. Lauren was writing about feminist issues – the plight of women in Iraq, for example – but she could not convince her uncle that there really wasn't a female audience in the USA for a profile on a European Formula One driver.

"The more 'get a pen' moments passed, the more distance there was between us. But we were always close in an almost sibling-like way."

Despite Opert's unrelenting fanatical belief that he knew what was right and best for other people, Lauren, like Derek and Nikolai, believes that he had a significant, positive impact on her life.

"I think that Fred was deeply influential in me developing a sense of myself, in that to be raised close to someone who lives life on their own terms, and who sees so much possibility in the world; who looks at the globe and sees it as something to explore fully and spontaneously; who didn't see anything barred to him, ever. That formed me radically – so, that could mean talking my way into a club, that could mean spontaneously buying a plane ticket, or doing something that someone else wouldn't think was even an option in their lives.

"I think that I developed a certain edge and a certain glamour, if I may say that. That would have just been something that existed in fiction, or in television, if I hadn't had Fred's influence in my life. I think that he's someone who possibly made New York feel possible to me instead of something that other people did.

"I think that just something about walking through the world as though you have a place in it. As though people are there to be met and charmed, and food is out there to be tasted, and music is out there to be heard. That way of living, I certainly gained that from my parents, but with Fred it was amplified in a certain way. And there was an edge to it that really appealed to me.

"You know, this notion that you didn't just have to do what you were supposed to be doing. And what that meant could take a lot of different forms and it could last through your whole life and it didn't just have to be an experimental adolescence, but a way of living a totally engaged life, a way of making the self, which interestingly enough are very feminist concepts and yet ones that I think I embody in part because Fred was the fast car in my life.

"From Fred I got an education in the possibilities of how to live that I think are incredibly rare in this world. Some of that was era specific, and some of that was who he got to be because of his race and gender and the time of a certain century in which he was born, but I think that he would have been him no matter what, and that helped me."

Opert had a need to influence people's lives. The members of his surrogate family are the most striking examples, along with some of his friends, but even with the young mechanics he hired and his business employees he sought to give advice and guidance. It seems that it was important for him to know that he was having an influence. His 'get a pen' moments were not limited to family and close friends.

Sasha Yanovich

Another person who Opert helped was a young woman called Sasha Yanovich, whose father was in the Yugoslav army and who had done business with Opert. During the civil war that ravaged that country, and eventually caused its breakup, Opert provided a safe home for Sasha and supported her while she studied at the University of Virginia.

She and Nikolai Koza were briefly together, but he lost touch with her when she completed her studies.

Fred's ex-wife, Sharon, summed up the balance that Opert was able to find for himself by establishing his surrogate family.

"You know the whole idea of a family and racing [was difficult], but I think he worked it out because he was a wonderful supporter of Nikolai. He even said to me on one of the last times I saw him, he came to Florida and we met at a University of Virginia Christmas Party, he said, 'You know, Nikolai is like the best son I could have had.' So, if he worked it out, if he was able to have a family and do racing at the same time, it was perfect."

The Last Weeks

In June 2016 Fred Opert persuaded a staff member at the Ridgewood Rehabilitation Center in New Jersey, where he was a patient, to drive to his house and pack a bag for him. He checked out of the centre and drove to Montreal for the seventh round of the 2016 Formula One world championship, where he met up with his nephew and racing buddy, Derek.

Opert's friend Nico Rosberg – the son of his old friend and protégé, the 1982 world champion Keke Rosberg – was fighting for the title against his teammate, three-time world champion Lewis Hamilton. Despite his deteriorating health, Fred desperately wanted to see Nico defeat Hamilton in Montreal and add more points to his championship lead.

Opert hadn't made a habit of attending Formula One races. As Keke Rosberg commented:

"He was not happy hanging around without any function ... I think only when Nico was driving did he attend F1 races as a fan, because also Eje [Elgh] was present in his [Marcus] Ericsson management role.

"You also need to remember F1 passes were not so easy to get hold of under Bernie's regime. He found to his surprise that Bernie did provide him with passes to most races he applied for. Not always though ..."

The state of Opert's health had been in a downward spiral for some time – he had undergone open-heart surgery six years earlier, he had diabetes, and he suffered kidney problems. He had also seriously damaged his feet while walking barefoot on hot asphalt in Florida; they never healed. He walked with great difficulty and resorted to the support of a walking frame. Even with this he could only walk for about 50 metres before he had to rest. Nikolai Koza also commented that his friend was very bad at taking his medication.

Close friend, Eje Elgh, remembers witnessing the decline in Opert's health.

"Unfortunately, I had the experience of seeing his health go down gradually but it accelerated, especially the last years, say 2014, '15, '16 ... For Fred there was nothing else in the world but F1 or motorsport, that was his life. He would do anything to go to races. Unfortunately, in the modern world of Formula One it became very hectic and very controlled, very different from what it used to be, and it became harder and harder to look after Fred because his mobility got more limited every year, so in the end he needed assistance. I did what I could, and I tried to arrange it. I discussed this with Keke a lot and I remember Keke, who had a more professional relationship with Fred than what I had, I was more just like the son, you know. I remember Keke was telling Fred in a letter, after we discussed it, saying: 'Fred, now you stay home until you are back on your feet, until you are stronger. It will be much easier for everybody.'

"But Fred couldn't resist, he was still making plans and, always in January, I had long emails and phone calls with Fred where he was telling me which races he wanted to go to, and where he would stay, and when we would meet, and could he come in my rental car and so on. It was simply his life. Now, unfortunately no one really knew that he was hiding his illness, but he was, and he wouldn't tell anyone."

But no one could tell Opert that he couldn't do something and so, despite his condition, his resolve to see Nico Rosberg win the F1 title was such that he had worked for many months in rehab so that he could make a trip to Europe. He was determined to do it. His schedule was to go to Hungary, then to Germany, then Greece for a one-week vacation at a friend's house on the island of Naxos, then back to US to return to rehab.

He had also booked tickets to fly to Austin Texas, Mexico and Brazil for the Grands Prix in those places.

The race in Montreal did nothing to lift his spirits as Nico Rosberg had a disastrous day with the two Mercedes once again colliding at the first corner. Rosberg only managed fifth place after a late-race spin while trying to pass Max Verstappen. Hamilton went on to win the race to take a significant chunk out of Rosberg's championship lead, leaving him with a slim nine-point margin.

Opert returned to the Ridgewood Rehabilitation Center only to check out again in July, against doctors' orders, to fly to Hungary for the Grand Prix on July 24th. Before he left the USA Fred stopped off at Colombia Presbyterian Hospital to see his cardiologist, Dr Lee. She was horrified and angry, but she knew Fred well enough to know that he would stick to any plan that he had already made to attend a race meeting.

"Fred, I can't believe you are going to Europe right now," was her bewildered comment.

Dr Lee advised Opert to get to a major, or teaching, hospital if he had problems, which she anticipated. Despite having to rely on a walking frame, he flew off to Budapest where he met up with Andreas Mann from Germany, his close friend of 25 years. Nico Rosberg had got a pass for Opert for the Hungarian race, and it seems likely that Eje Elgh provided one for Mann. At this stage Opert hadn't been provided with a pass for the German race on the following weekend.

Mann had to return to Germany for an appointment on the Monday after the Hungarian race, while Opert had booked to fly to Germany on Tuesday. When Mann tried to persuade Opert to change his flights, he couldn't understand his insistence to stay with his plan to fly, without help, on the Tuesday. Finally Opert revealed that he had made arrangements to meet with a lady friend on Monday. Budapest is famous for its spas and bath houses, and in true Opert fashion he had planned his rendezvous carefully. He arranged to meet the woman in a spa, explaining to Andreas that as he would already be in the water when the woman arrived she would not see the difficulties he suffered trying to walk.

Opert and Andreas attended qualifying for the Grand Prix where they watched Nico take pole position and where he met up with Nico for a drink. But on race day the Mercedes team doctor, Australian Dr Luke Bennett[1], noticed that Fred looked extremely unwell in the Mercedes hospitality area. Dr Bennett called an ambulance and accompanied Opert to the military hospital in Budapest. He suspected that Opert had a severe infection. He was concerned that, given his existing condition, an infection could be very dangerous. Dr Bennett sent a text to Georg Nolte, Nico's management and PR person, advising him of the situation. In turn, nolte sent texts to Opert's nephew, Derek, to keep him up to date. He also sent a photo that he had taken the day before of Opert and Nico together. Needless to say, Opert not only missed the race but also his date at the spa the following day.

Eje Elgh saw Opert for the last time in Hungary.

"The last time I met Fred was in Hungary about two or three weeks before he passed away, and he was in bad shape and I was really worried. I said, 'What's going on?' He said he wasn't well because of some medicine he had taken, but he would be fine the next day. But he was taken to hospital. It was very hot at the time in Budapest. I managed to call him, and I called Derek and I spoke to him. I was busy with my work at that time, but I was trying to see if I had to go to hospital to help him, but he said, 'No, no, it is no problem. It's just because I took the wrong medicine.' And he was convinced that he was going to go to Hockenheim."

In Hungary Nico Rosberg again failed to win the race. And for the first time that season he lost the lead of the championship after finishing second to his teammate.

Once again, against better advice, Opert discharged himself from hospital in Hungary to fly to Germany for the next Grand Prix at Hockenheim on July 31st. He flew into Frankfurt where Mann met him and took him to his home. His friends were very concerned about his condition, and, in an attempt to thwart Opert's plan to attend the Grand Prix, they told him that there were no passes available.

---

1   Dr Bennett originally specialised in intensive care and critical care before joining the Royal Flying Doctor Service in Western Australia. He indulged his passion for motorsport by working with track-side medical teams at the Australian Grand Prix, Australian World Rally Championship rounds, the Australasian Safari and other events.

Finally Keke Rosberg confronted Opert, telling him that he should go home to the USA to recover, then, if he was well enough, attend the US Grand Prix in Austin, Texas.

On Thursday July 28th Mann took Opert to the Mainz hospital, near Frankfurt airport, where he stayed until Thursday August 4th when Mann took him to Frankfurt airport, from where he flew back to the USA. Interestingly he had purchased a return ticket: Frankfurt to New York, and back to Frankfurt. Why is unknown. Other than to visit his friend, or pick up a car for export, there was no reason for Opert to return to Frankfurt; the F1 circus had already moved on, and he had already booked his trip to Greece.

Reine Wisell – who had been the Chevron works driver in the '70s, had driven for Opert in a Formula B Chevron at Sebring, and stayed with Opert and his wife Sharon – saw him in Germany: "Fred looked very bad. He was very ill, I think."

Opert's stubborn insistence on going to Europe had caused tension between family and friends, as his sister Judi desperately wanted Mann to send him home.

Being 24 years younger than Opert, Mann considered him like an older brother.

"Fred always had his way. The way he did things. He was the one who decided how he wanted things done. We were best friends for 25 years and when Fred asked me to do something I was happy to do it.

"Fred was always perfectly organised and he had his schedule and timing for everything. When he was with me in Europe he had already made his bookings for Greece and then three more rounds of the world championship in Austin in the USA, then Mexico and Brazil."

In Germany things hadn't got better for Nico Rosberg. On July 31st Lewis Hamilton took the lead from Rosberg at the start of the race then won the Grand Prix comfortably, with the German back in fourth and now 19 points behind in the championship battle.

From Germany Opert returned to his home in Ramsey, New Jersey. He planned to see his cardiologist then travel on to Greece, but the trips to follow Nico Rosberg's championship fortunes had taken their toll. A few days later the man who had been such an important part of motorsport in the USA, Canada, Europe, Mexico, South America, New Zealand and Japan, throughout the '60s, '70s and early '80s, died on August 9th 2016, at the age of 77.

Sadly, Opert didn't live to see Nico Rosberg fight back to win the world championship by five points, when he finished in second place in the final race of the season at Abu Dhabi.

Opert's choices in his last few months angered some members of his family and strained the relationship between family and friends. His sister Judi had pleaded with her brother not to go to Europe and his niece Lauren was angry about the choices that her uncle made in the last months of his life.

"Fred didn't spend time talking about his feelings. At the end he might have been in complete denial."

But Opert may not have been in denial; he rang his friend Nikolai Koza from Germany and told him, 'This could be my last Formula One race.' Perhaps he was referring simply to his increasing difficulty travelling and trying to get around, or perhaps he finally realised how ill he was. Nikolai was more philosophical about Opert's decisions: "Fred went out on his own terms."

Eje Elgh holds the view that Opert was hiding his condition, and perhaps he had an inkling that he was running out of time.

"Now, unfortunately no one really knew that he was hiding his illness, but he was, and he wouldn't tell anyone.

"When I think of Fred, I even think that he knew his time was up and he wanted to be in the Formula One paddock and that should be the last thing he did. He was very very fond of Nico, Keke's son, and I think if Fred had lived and seen Nico become world champion then somehow he would have gotten another ten years in life, because that was all he lived for at the time. But whatever, you know – he was denying his condition, sure – but likewise, knowing the problems that he had he was an incredible fighter ... he was fighting not only the doctors, he was fighting his sister and family, to the point where it became stupid, all in order to travel to go to F1 races. Still it was a sad way."

In line with Opert's wishes there was no memorial to celebrate his life and his ashes were scattered at Martha's Vineyard, a place he had loved and shared with his family.

Opert's niece, Lauren, commented on this:

"The family deliberated about a service, a memorial for Fred, but he was absolutely adamant about it, always.

"There has been a bit of closure that has been missing because of this. But he was absolutely insistent that there not be [a service]. I think in some respects it could be said that, 'Who cares if he didn't want this, it's for us.' But it was in writing. It was discussed extensively."

Opert's love of auto racing was the driving force of his life. He ran his businesses not for personal wealth, but to finance his involvement in motorsport. He eschewed love and marriage, favouring freedom to pursue his addiction to the adrenaline high of racing. His passion for racing was his raison d'être and ultimately hastened his death.

The following obituary appeared in *The New York Times*:

Frederic B. Opert, 77, died peacefully at his home in Ramsey, NJ, on August 9. In addition to operating an automotive dealership for fifty-five years, Fred owned racing teams that competed on four continents and was a successful racer in his own right. He was instrumental in forging the careers of over twenty Formula One drivers including several who became world champions. For that and more, Fred was widely celebrated for his instincts in discovering new drivers and developing their talent on the track. He was also one of the first Americans to manage a Formula One team. Fred lived every day as an adventure, on his own terms, until the last.

Beyond his lifelong friendships in the racing community, Fred's heart held room for the University of Virginia Cavaliers and the legacy of Thomas Jefferson, the sands of St. Martin, St. Tropez, Lucy Vincent, and Palm Beach, where he also resided, the music of Chet Baker and the Rolling Stones, the films and plays of Martin Scorsese and David Mamet, German engineering, French women, American sports, the timeless style of white slacks paired with a blue shirt, and the kids he took such pride in watching grow up. Most of all he loved his friends and family.

Acknowledgements

I met Fred Opert once in 1977. A group of us had gone to Fred's room at the Travelodge hotel overlooking Auckland harbour in New Zealand. It was the year that Opert brought out the Finns, Rosberg and Kozarowitzky, to race in the Peter Stuyvesant Series. Keke Rosberg won the championship and repeated the effort the following year. The Opert cars were always immaculate, and Opert and his drivers really enjoyed their time in New Zealand. As it happens, Opert's cars were Chevrons, built in the Lancashire town of Bolton, in the UK, where I was born.

Fast forward to August 2017. I was writing a blog post about a friend's historic Chevron racing car when I discovered that it had been originally imported into the USA by Fred Opert. Then I discovered that Fred had died one year earlier. More research revealed that there was very little information about the man, which struck me as strange given his achievements and personality.

With the help of the internet, I managed to find Fred's sister, Judi Sandler, and her husband Jim. They told me that no one had written about Fred, and they had no objection to me taking on the project. Later I got to talk to other members of Fred's family: brother Larry, niece Lauren and nephew Derek. They were friendly and patient sources of all manner of information about Fred. An accomplished author, Lauren provided valuable advice.

But my first port of call was my Kiwi connections. I emailed race driver and engineer Garry Pedersen to tell him what I had in mind. Before I even received his reply, emails from NZ mechanics Barry and Ross Sale arrived and the flood gates were opened. It turned out that Fred Opert employed a large number of Kiwis and Aussies. All the ones I made contact with were happy to help, and full of great anecdotes. So, thanks to: Garry Pedersen, the Sale brothers, Dave McMillan, Tom Hooker, Barry Green, Dick Bennetts, Bernie Ferri, and 'Wombat' Devereux. Their lives have been so interesting, I could have written a story about each of these men from 'Down Under.'

Each call I made created another call, and the snowball grew as it gathered pace. I knew there were many racing drivers who would be able to give me insight into Fred, but I thought it might be difficult to get some of these busy and famous people to spend time chatting with me. Fortunately Fred was a popular person and, luckily for me, everyone wanted to tell me a story. So, thanks to Fred's close friends Eje Elgh and Keke Rosberg, and to: Nico Rosberg (and his delightful Executive Assistant Lucy Earlam), Alan Jones, Bobby Rahal, Howden Ganley, Tim Schenken, Brian Redman,

Acknowledgements

Héctor Rebaque, Bobby Brown, Reine Wisell, Nick Craw, John Bisignano, Freddy van Beuren, Marco Tolama, 'Wink' Bancroft, John Powell, Tom Davey, Jim Crawley, and Carl Liebich.

Brian Robertson should be in that list of drivers, having made a habit of winning, and in the process taking the Canadian championship. But because Brian was also Fred's business partner for many years, running Fred Opert Canada, he gets a special mention. For a long time, Brian was elusive, but when I did manage to track him down he added more colour to my picture of Fred.

Fred Schuchard got to know Fred in the very early days when he was an agent for Elva Courier sports cars. He wrote about their friendship then shared with me his memories of Fred's early business, the New York Auto Show, and the establishment of Fred Opert Racing Enterprises.

Then there were Fred's American employees: Rick Mansfield (who even sent me 1960s Opert calendars and race suit patches), John Leotta, Rich Jacksic, Duncan Pitcairn, Pete McCarthy, Mark Coughlin, Joe Grimaldi, Frank DelVecchio, and the women who provided a female view into what was primarily a man's world: Linda Graham and Judy Stropus.

Speaking of the women who have helped me, Fred's wife of five years, Sharon Seagren, provided a delightful insight into her time with Fred, their whirlwind marriage, the fun times they enjoyed, and their friendship in the later years of Fred's life. And I was able to track down Rabbi 'Buz' Bogage, who married Sharon and Fred, and who proved to be an entertaining character.

Fred was the North American importer of Chevron race cars. Neil Bailey, Steve Sheldon and Kevin Hodgkinson – who worked at Chevron when Fred was a regular visitor, then had his Formula Two team at the factory – helped with information, as did Tim Coleman who owns Chevron Heritage in the UK. Hodgkinson, the author of *In the Mind's Eye*, a book about Chevron racing cars, also supplied photos, some of which were given to him by Opert. Kevin's American friend, Lee Lubowski, provided the great shot of Opert with Tambay, Jones and Dolhem. Fellow Englishman David Williamson was able to fill me in on the last years of Fred's racing business, and the brief but ill-fated time when Fred was manager of the F1 team, ATS.

Fred dealt with many people in the motor racing business, two of the most important to his racing operations were Len Manley of Valvoline and John Hogan of Marlboro. They were both generous with their time, providing precious information.

Without the co-operation of Fred's 'family' this book would have been impossible. Beyond his normal family, he had others who were so close to him they were part of an extended family, including Nikolai Koza and Dr Andreas Mann, both of whom were able to give me unique insights into parts of Fred's life.

When it came to 'heavy' research, two people helped enormously: Allen Brown of oldracingcars.com and David Gordon, the author of *Chevron – The Derek Bennett*

153

Story, who interviewed Fred in October 1989 and allowed me to use quotations from that interview. My USA friend Lynne Huntting, aka PressSnoop, came to my aid on a couple of occasions; it seems there is no one involved in motorsport in the USA she doesn't know or can't find. Photographer Ross Cammick generously allowed me to use his photos from the NZ Peter Stuyvesant Series.

Nic Brasch, the Chair of Writers Victoria, who doesn't know one end of a racing car from the other, patiently reviewed my manuscript. His suggestions were invaluable and led to a restructure and some drastic cuts. His comment, "Just because it happened doesn't make it interesting," rings in my ears. John Holmes, editor of *Bespoke* magazine – who definitely does know about racing cars – kindly reviewed my manuscript.

Of course there is a special thank you for my wife, Sandra, who patiently lived through my mental absences when I was plotting some new requirement for the book, and was constantly regaled with my latest Fred Opert story.

If I've missed anyone I apologise. No one has been omitted intentionally, so either my system or my memory will be to blame.

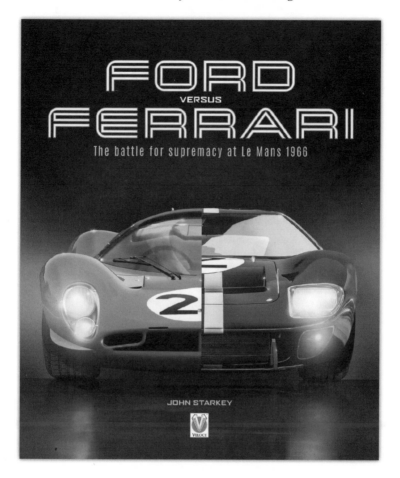

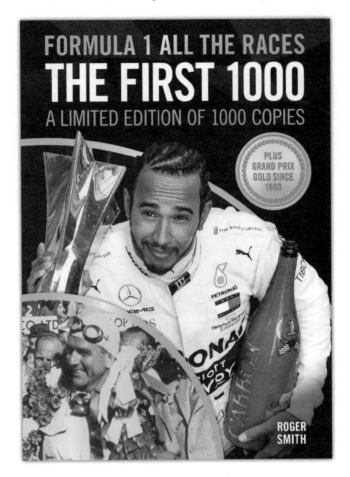

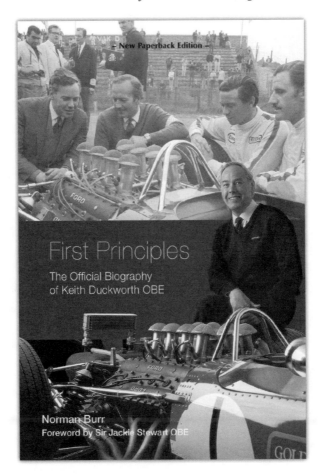

First Principles – The Official Biography of Keith Duckworth OBE
Norman Burr

This book chronicles the life of Keith Duckworth OBE, the remarkable engineer, co-founder of Cosworth Engineering and creator of the most successful F1 engine of all time, the DFV. This is a rounded look at the life and work of the man – work which included significant contributions to aviation, motorcycling, and powerboating.

ISBN: 978-1-787111-03-5
Paperback • 23.2x15.5cm • 352 pages • 200 pictures

For more information and price details, visit our website at www.veloce.co.uk
email: info@veloce.co.uk • Tel: +44(0)1305 260068

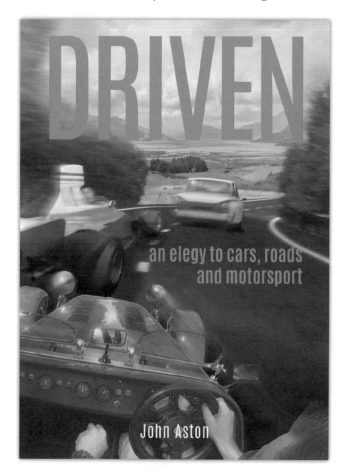

Driven – an elegy to cars, roads and motorsport
John Aston

John Aston's anecdotes, wit, strong opinion and acute observations recount insightful and affectionate portraits of the many facets of motor sport, its people and its places. DRIVEN takes you on a journey from Lake District vintage car trials to drag racing at Santa Pod, NASCAR racing in North Carolina and international events at Silverstone.

ISBN: 978-1-787114-39-5
Paperback • 21x14.8cm • 272 pages

For more information and price details, visit our website at www.veloce.co.uk • email: info@veloce.co.uk • Tel: +44(0)1305 260068

Index